An Introduction to Chromebook Computing

Jim Gatenby

BERNARD BABANI (publishing) LTD
The Grampians
Shepherds Bush Road
London W6 7NF
England

www.babanibooks.com

i

Please Note

Although every care has been taken with the production of this book to ensure that all information is correct at the time of writing and that any projects, designs, modifications and/ or programs, etc., contained herewith, operate in a correct and safe manner and also that any components specified are normally available in Great Britain, the Publishers and Author do not accept responsibility in any way for the failure (including fault in design) of any project, design, modification or program to work correctly or to cause damage to any equipment that it may be connected to or used in conjunction with, or in respect of any other damage or injury that may be so caused, nor do the Publishers accept responsibility in any way for the failure to obtain specified components.

Notice is also given that if equipment that is still under warranty is modified in any way or used or connected with home-built equipment then that warranty may be void.

British Library Cataloguing in Publication Data:

A catalogue record for this book is available from the British Library

ISBN 978-0-85934-777-8

Cover Design by Gregor Arthur

Printed and bound in Great Britain for Bernard Babani (publishing) Ltd

About this Book

Chromebooks are made by several major computer manufacturers and, unlike other laptops, Chromebooks work mainly on the Internet rather than using their own internal resources. This book is intended to help with this new approach to computing. If you are new to computing, Essential Jargon is explained on pages (x)-(xii).

The first chapter describes the many uses of Chromebooks and the vast amount of excellent free software.

The technical specification of Chromebooks is explained in plain English, together with the various external accessories available. Also using the touchpad or a mouse to operate the Chromebook.

Setting up and connecting to Wi-Fi and creating a Google Account are then covered, followed by a tour of the main screens, the pre-installed apps (or programs), the settings icons and downloading, installing and managing apps.

The Chrome Browser is the user-interface for the Chromebook and using it to search for information is described, together with Incognito or Private Browsing and Browsing as a Guest. This is followed by the use of major software apps, free with the Chromebook, i.e. Google Docs, Sheets and Slides. Also covered is saving your work as files, managing them online and offline as is printing and compatibility with Microsoft Word, Excel and PowerPoint.

Finally, communication with email and Google Hangouts is covered, followed by eBooks, movies and TV, including connecting to a large screen and Bluetooth headphones, etc.

I have found the Chromebook to be an excellent innovation compared with more traditional laptops. It is faster, easier to use, has much longer battery life and is available at very low prices. The Chromebook is also designed to keep your programs and data more secure than traditional computers.

About the Author

Jim Gatenby trained as a Chartered Mechanical Engineer and initially worked at Rolls-Royce Ltd using computers in the analysis of jet engine performance. He obtained a Master of Philosophy degree in Mathematical Education by research at Loughborough University of Technology and taught mathematics and computing in school for many years before becoming a full-time author. His most recent teaching posts included Head of Computer Studies and Information Technology Coordinator. The author has written over forty books in the fields of educational computing and Microsoft Windows, as well as several titles for Android tablets and smartphones. (The Google Chromebook is a close relative of Android devices).

The author has considerable experience of teaching students of all ages and abilities, in school and in adult education. For several years he successfully taught the well-established CLAIT course and also GCSE Computing and Information Technology.

Trademarks

Google, Google Drive, Google Chrome, Chrome OS, Gmail, Google Sheets, Google Docs, Google Slides, Hangouts, Google Keep, Google Cloud Print and YouTube are trademarks or registered trademarks of Google, Inc. Microsoft Windows, Microsoft Word, Microsoft Excel and PowerPoint are trademarks or registered trademarks of Microsoft Corporation. All other brand and product names used in this book are recognized as trademarks or registered trademarks, of their respective companies.

Acknowledgements

I would like to thank my wife Jill for her support during the preparation of this book and also Michael Babani for making the project possible.

Contents

5

The Chrome Browser   47

9

Essential Jargon

Software

The *programs*, i.e. sets of instructions or *statements*, which tell a computer what to do. Statements are *coded* in a programming language such as JavaScript or Python.

System software includes the *Operating System (OS)* which controls the basic running of a computer. *Applications software* or *apps* are programs to do a particular task of your choice such as editing a photo or playing music.

File

A *data file* contains information such as a list of names, a text document or a *spreadsheet* (a table of figures). A *program file* contains statements or instructions which can be *executed* or run by a computer.

Hardware

This refers to the physical components of a computer such as the screen, keyboard, mouse, memory, hard drives, etc.

Internal Storage vs RAM

Internal Storage is memory in a computer in which apps and data files are permanently saved until they are deleted by the user or overwritten with later versions. Many computers now use *SSDs (Solid State Drives)* for Internal Storage. An SSD is *flash memory*, having no moving parts.

Apps and data in the *RAM (Random Access Memory)*, are *volatile* i.e. deleted whenever the computer is switched off.

External Storage

This refers to *removable* devices like *external hard drives*, and *flash drives/memory sticks*, discussed on page 16.

The CPU (Central Processing Unit)

Often referred to as the "brains" of a computer, the CPU fetches the instructions for the current program from the RAM then carries them out or executes them.

The Internet and World Wide Web

The *Internet* is a global *network of networks*, connecting millions of computers by Wi-Fi, etc. The *World Wide Web* is millions of *Web pages* of information on *Web servers* (powerful computers run by large computer companies).

Web Browser

This is an app such as Google Chrome, Firefox, Safari and Internet Explorer, used to view Web pages after a *search* using a *search engine* such as Google.

Cloud Computing

This is the use of Internet *Web servers*, discussed above, to store data and run our programs, accessed by Google Chrome from our own computers, known as *Web clients*.

Units of Data Storage

A *byte* is a group of 8 *bits* or *binary digits* **0** and **1**, used to represent the *digits 0-9*, a *letter* of the alphabet or an *instruction*. For example, the letter **C** would be stored as **01000011** in binary. The following terms are used for different amounts of data.

> 1 Kilobyte (KB)   = 1024 Bytes
> 1 Megabyte (MB) = 1024 Kilobytes
> 1 Gigabyte (GB) = 1024 Megabytes
> 1 Terabyte (TB) = 1024 Gigabytes

User Interface

This is the way we interact with a computer and includes hardware such as the keyboard, touchpad or mouse and the various screen displays or *desktop*s containing *icons* and *menus*. Icons are small images on the screen which can be selected or clicked to launch an application such as a Web browser. A menu displays a list of clickable options.

The Chromebook and its Applications

Introduction

The Chromebook was launched in 2011 and introduced some major design features compared with other laptops. Its name is derived from the fact that it's a *notebook computer* (another name for a laptop) based on the *Google Chrome Web browser* and the *Google Chrome Operating System (OS)*. The Chromebook is designed to work mainly in the Clouds on the Internet. So most of the files you produce, such as photos and documents, are securely stored away from your computer in Cloud storage systems such as Google Drive, Dropbox, iCloud and Microsoft OneDrive.

Acer Chromebook 14

While the Chromebook is a relative newcomer in the UK, it's a serious rival to Apple and Microsoft in the USA and dominates the educational market there.

Typical Uses of a Chromebook

Some typical tasks include:

- Creating and editing text documents and financial spreadsheets for personal, work or educational use.

- Searching the Web for information on any subject and displaying Web pages for educational, professional or leisure purposes.

- Importing, viewing and editing photographs.

- Drawing and painting.

- Sending and receiving e-mails.

- Using social networks, such as Facebook, Twitter, and Instagram.

- Reading online editions of newspapers, magazines and *eBooks*.

- Listening to music, radio, watching videos, YouTube. Watching live and catch up TV.

- Mirroring your Chromebook screen on a Television using Chromecast, Miracast or HDMI.

- Looking at maps, including Google Maps, Google Earth and Google Street View.

- Buying goods online, booking holidays and flights.

- Managing your online bank account and finances.

- Playing games from the Chrome Web Store and Google Play Store.

Chromebook Software

Notes on the jargon used for different types of software are given on page (xi) near the front of this book. Software used on a Chromebook consists of:

- The *Chrome OS* operating system.
- The *Chrome Web Browser*.
- Popular *apps pre-installed* on a new Chromebook and apps that you have installed from the *Google Play Store* or the *Chrome Web Store*.

Chrome OS vs The Chrome Web Browser

- Chrome OS is pre-installed on the Internal Storage of a new Chromebook.
- Chrome OS manages the basic functions on a Chromebook, such as screen display, desktop, etc.
- The Chrome Web browser also acts as the user interface to run *Web-based apps*.
- *Web-based apps* are programs stored and executed on Web servers in the Clouds.
- Most, but not all, icons in your **ALL APPS** screen are simply *links* to run *Web-based apps* in the Clouds.

Chrome OS Security

Chrome OS is regarded as more secure than other operating systems. *Security updates* are installed *automatically*, applications run in a closed, protected environment called a *sandbox* and data is *encrypted* or encoded so that hackers can't read it. Also the Chromebook uses a *Verified Boot* which checks the system on startup and automatically corrects any corruption due to malware or hackers, etc.

.

Pre-installed Apps

After a new user signs up for a Google account, as discussed in Chapter 3, a number of apps already appear as icons on the **ALL APPS** screen, as shown below.

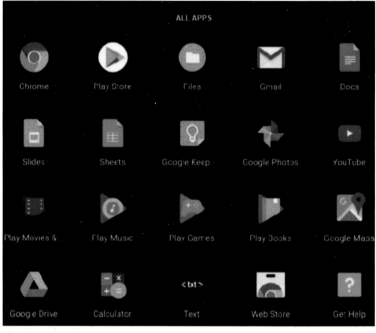

The Chromebook All Apps Screen

These icons are the same or very similar, to the icons for the same apps on Android smartphones and tablets. As discussed in Chapter 4, the apps pre-installed on a new computer, shown above, can be supplemented by installing apps from the Play Store and from the Chrome Web Store.

These icons represent popular applications which can be launched and executed by clicking or tapping their icon.

The pre-installed apps cover many of the important and popular activities on the Chromebook. Some of the main applications are discussed below and on the next two pages

Chrome

Google Chrome is a *Web browser*, used to display Web pages and to navigate between pages using *links*. You can also revisit Web pages from your *browsing history* or which you've *bookmarked* for future viewing.

Play Store

The **Play Store** gives access to a huge number of *Android apps* in different categories, now available for the Chromebook. These are free or can be bought online for a few pounds.

Files

Files is an application used to *manage files* such as documents or photos. It can also be used to *copy files* between Google Drive in the Clouds and your Internal Storage or External Storage.

Gmail

Google mail or **Gmail** is a free e-mail service for sending and receiving messages consisting of text, pictures and *attached files*.

Docs

Docs is the Google Drive word processing program and has many features similar to the very popular Microsoft Word. Documents are automatically stored in Google Drive in the Clouds and can also be saved in the Microsoft Word *file format*.

Slides

Slides is a Chromebook program, similar to Microsoft PowerPoint, allowing you to give a slide show or illustrate a talk or lecture to an audience using text, photos or videos on a large screen.

Sheets

Sheets is Google's answer to Microsoft Excel, the leading *spreadsheet* program. It is used for calculations on tables of figures for financial, scientific or other purposes and greatly speeds up otherwise lengthy and complex tasks.

Google Keep

Google Keep is used to make quick notes for study, in the home or at work. Can include pictures and videos. Share notes with friends via Google Drive and the Clouds.

Google Photos

Google Photos saves and organizes all the photos you take using the built-in Webcam on the Chromebook. Photos are automatically *backed up* to Google Drive in the Clouds and can be *edited* and *shared* with friends.

YouTube

YouTube is a Website used by individuals and companies to upload and share videos for other people to view. These may include amusing incidents or popular music videos.

Play Movies & TV

Play Movies & TV is used to download and watch videos and TV shows bought from the Play Store.

Play Music

Play Music allows you to shop for music to save and organize in playlists.

Play Games

Play Games is used to install games from the Chrome Web Store and the Android Play Store.

Play Books

Use **Play Books** to read *ebooks* in your **Library** or download new ones from a choice of millions in the Play Store, some of them free.

Google Maps

Google Maps displays maps from all over the world including travel times, the current weather, details of your current location and traffic news.

Google Drive

Google Drive is used to upload and download files to and from the Clouds and view them on any computer connected to the Internet. Also used as an automatic backup system. 15GB of free storage with another 100GB for 2 years, (which must be claimed).

Web Store

The **Web Store** contains apps and *extensions* (small programs designed to give extra functions to the Chrome Web browser).

Web-based Apps

Most Chromebook apps or programs are not actually saved on the Internal Storage on your device. Instead the apps themselves exist only on *Web servers* in the Clouds.

To verify this, you can switch off your Wi-Fi (as discussed on page 31) so you have no connection to the Internet. The icons on your **ALL APPS** screen still appear as shown on page 4. However, clicking an icon such as the **Play Store** opens only empty boxes, as shown in the sample on the left below. The online version of the same **Play Store** sample, complete with the two games' images is shown on the right.

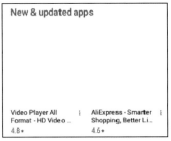

Play Store Offline   Play Store Online

When you run a Web-based app with Wi-Fi On, it is actually being executed on a Web server on the Internet, with the Chrome Web browser acting as the user interface.

The icons on the **ALL APPS** screen shown on page 4 are merely *links* to launch the apps or programs in the Chrome Web browser. Also to display on your local Chromebook screen, the results of the Web-based program execution.

So these Web-based apps can only be run when you are *online*, i.e. connected to the Internet.

Web-based apps include word processors, spreadsheets, online shopping, form filling, games and e-mails. Examples include Google Docs and Sheets and Microsoft 365 (Word, Excel, PowerPoint, etc.), discussed later in this book.

The Cloud-based approach is the main idea behind the Chromebook. As well as running programs and storing data in the Clouds, the Clouds are now the main source of new software. Previously, new software was bought on discs and CDs and copied onto your computer's hard drive. Installing software from the Clouds is quicker, easier and ensures it is up-to-date.

So the Chromebook can be as productive as much bigger, heavier and more expensive laptop and desktop computers.

Offline Apps

There may be times when you want to use your Chromebook where there is no Internet. As already stated, the Chromebook is essentially a Web-based computer. However, there are some tasks which can be carried out offline, including the following:

- Editing documents and spreadsheets created in Google Docs and Sheets and MS Word and Excel.

- Watching Movies and TV that have been downloaded and saved previously on your Internal Storage when you were online.

- Listening to Music.

- Playing certain games and apps that run offline.

- Reading and replying to your Gmail messages. Replies are sent next time you're online.

- Editing photos.

Advantages of the Chromebook

This Cloud-based approach of the Chromebook brings many advantages:

- Chromebooks don't need bulky *hard disk drives* or *SSDs (Solid State Drives)* for storing software and data files. They are therefore cheaper and slimmer than traditional laptops.

- The simple components of the Chromebook are less demanding on the battery. (10-13 hours between charges compared with 1- 6 hours on some laptops.)

- If more storage is needed, full size *USB ports* allow cheap flash drives and external hard drives to be added by simply plugging in, as shown on page 17.

- A Chromebook can be used for entertainment such as social networking, TV, movies, etc., video games or serious work such as e-mails, browsing the Web, word processing, spreadsheets and editing photos.

- *Online*, i.e. *Web-based*, versions of leading software such as Microsoft Word and Excel are available as well as Google's own excellent Docs and Sheets word processing and spreadsheet software.

- The design of the Chromebook and Chrome Web browser make it less susceptible to viruses and other types of malware.

- Over a million *Android apps* in the Google Play Store can also be installed and used on later versions of the Chromebook.

Chromebook Specifications

Introduction

Chromebooks are produced by many well-known companies such as Asus, Acer, Dell, Samsung, Toshiba, HP and Lenovo. Listed below is a typical Chromebook specification. The technical terms are explained on pages (xi and xii) and discussed further on pages 13-15.

Operating System	Chrome OS
CPU	Intel Celeron
RAM	2GB or 4GB
Internal Storage	16GB, 32GB or 64GB (SSD or eMMC)
Screen size	11.6 –15.6 inches
Touchscreen	Available on some Chromebooks
Sound	2 stereo speakers
Connectivity	Wi-Fi
	Bluetooth
	3.5mm Audio Jack
	Charging port
	HDMI port
	USB ports (2)
Battery life	10 -13 hours
Camera	HD Webcam

The Chromebook Specification in Detail

- *Chrome OS* is the Google Chrome Operating System, which is based on the *Chrome Web browser* and the *Linux operating system*.

- *The CPU (Central Processing Unit)* shown on page 11 and discussed on page (xii) is crucial to the speed of a computer. The Intel Celeron processor listed on page 11 is fitted to many other laptop computers.

- *2GB* of *RAM* (RAM is discussed on page (xi)) shown on page 11 should be enough for general work.

- The *Internal Storage* of 16GB, 32GB or 64GB is low compared with most laptop and desktop computers having 500GB or perhaps 1TB. This accounts for the low price, low weight and thin size of Chromebooks.

- The Internal Storage can be supplemented by up to 115GB of Google Drive Cloud Storage (page 15) and also by removable storage as discussed on page 16.

- *eMMC* is a type of Internal Storage *flash memory*. Cheaper and slower than SSD, discussed on page (xi).

- The cheapest Chromebooks at around £150 have 2GB of RAM and 16GB Internal Storage. This should be adequate for word processing, spreadsheets, e-mail, Web browsing and student coursework, etc.

- For more demanding work involving videos, games or graphics, etc., you might pay about £270 for 4GB of RAM and 32GB Internal Storage or about £500 for 4GB of RAM and 64GB of Internal Storage.

Connectivity

- *Wi-Fi* listed on page 11 allows the Chromebook to be connected to the Internet via a home or office *network router*, *public Wi-Fi* or *mobile hotspot* (discussed later in this book).

- *Bluetooth* listed on page 11 is a technology which connects devices, such as headphones, mice and keyboards to a computer over short distances.

- Some Chromebooks have an *HDMI (High Definition Multimedia Interface)* port, as shown below, to allow video *streaming* on the Chromebook to be viewed on a television.

- *USB (Universal Serial Bus)* ports on the side of a Chromebook, as shown below, allow all sorts of external devices to be connected, like a mouse or printer and external storage such as an SD card, microSD card, removable hard drive or SSD.

- A hole is provided on some Chromebooks to allow a *Kensington Lock* to be fitted. This device allows the Chromebook to be securely anchored by a strong cable to an immovable, heavy object such as a table.

Kensington   USB Ports   HDMI Port
Lock Hole

Ports on an Acer Chromebook 14

- A standard *audio* or *headset port*, also known as a *3.5mm stereo jack*, is normally built into a Chromebook, together with two *stereo speakers*.
- A battery charger port is provided to allow the charging cable to be inserted.

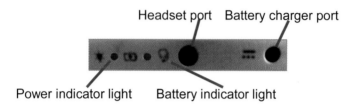

- The power indicator light on my Acer is blue when the Chromebook is switched On.
- The battery indicator light on my Acer is amber when charging and blue when the battery is fully charged
- The Webcam on the Chromebook is usually located in the centre of the frame or *bezel* at the top of the screen, as shown below. This allows you to take photos, make videos and have online chats with friends and relatives.
- A microphone is also built into the top of the screen, on the left or right of the Webcam.

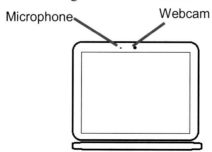

Extra Storage Space
Google Drive Cloud Storage

The Internal Storage space of 16-64GB on the Chromebook is relatively low compared with the 500GB or 1TB generally provided on laptop and desktop computers. This is compensated for by the fact that the Chromebook is designed to work mainly in the Clouds on the Internet with an initial 15GB of Google Drive Cloud storage, provided with a new Google Drive account, on any device. However, a further *100GB of free Cloud storage* is available for new Chromebook purchasers to claim, as discussed in Chapter 8. This is available for two years, after which you must delete files back to the nominal 15GB or make monthly payments to keep using the 100GB or step up to 1TB

Removable Storage: Using an SD Card Slot

If you want more local storage space, some Chromebooks have *built-in slots* for *microSD cards* or *SD cards* to store files such as photos, documents and spreadsheets.

SD card   microSD card   Adapter

The SD card and microSD card above are shown approximately full size. The *adapter* on the right allows a microSD card to be used in a full size SD card slot.

- *SD (Secure Digital)* cards are also used in digital cameras, allowing the transfer of photos between devices.

- *microSD* cards are widely used in smartphones.

- Both SD cards and microSD cards are available in sizes ranging from 32GB in increments up to 256GB.

Removable Storage: Using USB Ports

The USB ports on a Chromebook can be used to provide extra plug-in storage for your files such as documents and photos, etc. These storage devices are shown on page 17 and include:

- An *SD card reader*. Especially useful if your Chromebook doesn't have a built-in SD card slot. Can accommodate both SD and microSD cards. These can be bought for under £10.

- A *USB flash drive*, also known as a *memory stick*. Uses *flash memory*, allowing data to be saved, retrieved or deleted. Typical prices are £7 for a 16GB flash drive and £28 for 128GB.

- An *external hard drive* or an *external SSD* can be plugged into the USB port on a Chromebook. Hard drives range from about £23 for 300GB of storage, £50 for a 1TB drive up to a massive 10TB for about £260. 300GB should be more than enough for the average home user or student. External SSDs are more expensive than hard drives with a 500 GB SSD costing about £150.

Removable storage such as SD and microSD cards, flash drives and external disk drives can be useful when working with files in places where there is no Wi-Fi access to the Clouds. Also, important files or irreplaceable photos should be backed up on removable storage and saved in a safe place for extra security.

Files can be copied to and from the external storage using "drag and drop" or "cut and paste" methods as discussed later. For tasks like this, you may prefer to use a plug-in *mouse* rather than the built-in *touchpad.* Inexpensive mice, either cabled or wireless, are easily plugged into a USB port on the Chromebook and work straightaway. Similarly you may wish to connect a USB keyboard or an HDMI TV or monitor (discussed in Chapter 9).

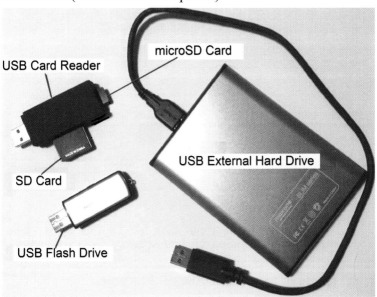

Removable USB Storage Devices

The Chromebook Keyboard

The keyboard has most of the keys of the standard QWERTY layout, but with some special function keys. These are discussed in more detail in Chapter 5.

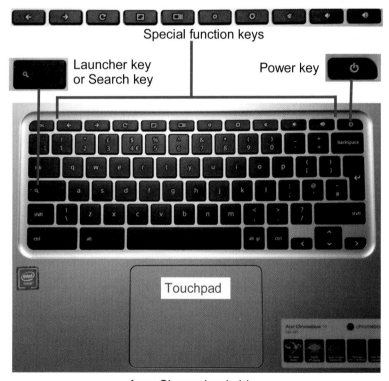

Acer Chromebook 14

The **Launcher key** or **Search key** shown above is used to open the **Launcher** screen to start searching the Internet with Google or to open the **ALL APPS** screen.

The **Power key** shown above is used to switch the Chromebook On and Off.

The Chromebook Touchpad

Whereas a lot of touchpads on laptops have a left and right button, the touchpad on the Chromebook is just one large, single button. However, as discussed shortly, you can still use the single-button touchpad on the Chromebook to replicate the actions possible with a mouse.

Alternatively, as discussed earlier, it's a cheap and easy job to connect a *wireless mouse* to a Chromebook. Simply plug the *wireless receiver* provided with the mouse into a USB port on the Chromebook (as shown on page 13). The mouse should work straightaway. For some of us, using the mouse may be preferable to using the touchpad when working on a desk or flat surface in the home, school, college or office. However, the mouse is not really very practical when you're working with the Chromebook on your lap. So it's worth being familiar with the Chromebook touchpad gestures, and their mouse equivalents, as follows:

Select an icon or menu item (Left-click with a mouse)

- Move the cursor across the screen to the required object by sliding a finger across the touchpad.

- Press a finger anywhere on the touchpad.

Open a Menu (Right-click with a mouse)

- As above but press down on the touchpad with <u>two</u> fingers instead of one.

- Alternatively, hold down the **Alt** key on the keyboard and press down on the touchpad with one finger.

Scroll the display (Middle mouse button/scroll wheel)

- Press two fingers and slide them over the touchpad, up and down or left and right as required.

Drag and Drop (Click and hold the left mouse button, then drag the item and release)

As discussed later, this action is used to copy a *file* from one location such as the **Google Drive** *folder* in the Clouds and save the file in another location, such as the **Downloads** folder on your Chromebook's Internal Storage.

- Slide the cursor over the file and touch and hold a finger on the touchpad.
- Slide a second finger over the touchpad to move the item to its new location or folder.
- Release both fingers to save the file in its new folder.

Touchscreen Gestures

If you have a Chromebook with a touchscreen, some common gestures are:

Select an icon or menu item (Left-click with a mouse)

- Tap with your finger the item you wish to select.

Open a menu (Right-click with a mouse)

- Tap and hold until the menu opens.

Scroll the display (Middle mouse button/scroll wheel)

- Slide or drag a finger left, right, up or down.

Please Note:

In the remainder of the this book, *click* is used to mean clicking with the left mouse button, pressing a finger on the touchpad or tapping on a touchscreen.

Right-click is used to mean clicking the right mouse button, pressing two fingers on the touchpad or tapping and holding a touchscreen.

Getting Started

Introduction

As discussed earlier, the Chromebook relies heavily on the Internet for many of its activities. If you are new to computing and setting up a new Chromebook in the home, you will need to create an account with an *Internet Service Provider (ISP)* such as BT, for a monthly fee. They normally provide a free *Wi-Fi Broadband Router* - a box to which you can connect several computers *wirelessly*. The router is connected by a cable to a domestic telephone socket and then to the Internet via the telephone network.

During the setup process you will need the *name* of your network, also known as the *SSID* (*Service Set Identifier*). This usually appears on a label at the back of the router, together with the network *password*.

If you are setting up a Chromebook in an office, school, college, hotel, etc., the router/network should already be set up. However, you will still need to obtain the network name/SSID and the password from the network manager.

Some more expensive Chromebooks have the in-built technology to connect to the Internet like a smartphone, via a *3G/4G* (and soon *5G*) *phone network* instead of a router.

Tethering

This enables you to use a computer in places where there is no Wi-Fi network. The Chromebook is connected wirelessly to a smartphone and accesses the Internet via the cell phone network. The phone is known as a *mobile hotspot*. Tethering is discussed further on page 106.

Connecting to Wi-Fi

- Press the **Power key** shown on page 18.

- Click to select your language and keyboard type and then click **Let's go** to open **Connect to network**.

- You are presented with a list of nearby Wi-Fi networks, including your own, such as **BTHub5-9CHT** in the example below.

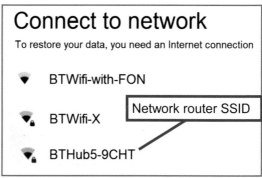

Getting Online to the Internet

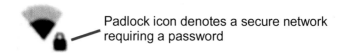

Padlock icon denotes a secure network requiring a password

- Click your network and then enter the network *password*, normally on the back of the Wi-Fi router.

- Click **Connect** to join the Wi-Fi network.

- Click **Next** and then **Accept and continue** to accept the Google Chrome OS Terms.

The Google Account

A Google Account is necessary to access all of Google's services, such as the Play Store, Gmail, Google Cloud Print, etc., as discussed later. If you've not already got a Google Account, you will need to create one, as follows:

- Click **More options** and then select **Create account**. Then enter your **First name** and **Last name** followed by your **Birthday** and **Gender**. After clicking **Next,** enter your e-mail address such as:

    stellajohnson@gmail.com

    (**@gmail.com** is already entered automatically)

- Click **Next**, then enter and confirm a strong **Password** consisting of at least 8 characters.

- Finally enter your phone number. This may be used, amongst other things, to reset your password.

- A *6-digit verification code* is sent to your phone for you to enter into the Chromebook.

- You are asked to agree to Google's terms and conditions before clicking **Create Account**.

- You are thanked by Google and invited to take a tour of the Chromebook features.

Already a Google Account Holder?

- If you already have a Google Account, it will take the form: **jimsmith@gmail.com**

- After joining the Wi-Fi network as discussed on page 22, enter your **Email Address**, in the format shown above, followed by **Next** and then enter your **Password**.

- After agreeing to accept Google's terms and conditions, etc., you are given the chance to take a tour of the Chromebook's apps and services.

- If you've previously stored files such as photos and documents in the Clouds in **Google Drive** on another computer such as a Windows PC or an iPad, these are available on any computer with an Internet connection and with **Google Drive** installed. So all your previous photos, documents, etc., will be accessible to your new Chromebook.

- **Google Drive** is discussed in detail later in this book.

Exploring the Chromebook Desktop

Tap the cross at the top right of the tour window to close the tour and display the *Chromebook Desktop* shown below. This is the screen you see when you start a new session. The background or **Wallpaper** shown below is just one example and can easily be changed as discussed in Chapter 4.

Shelf

The Shelf

This is the bar which appears along the bottom of the screen, as shown above and below. The **Shelf** contains the **Launcher button**, icons for **Pinned apps** and the **Status area** shown below. These features are discussed on the next few pages.

Launcher button   Pinned apps   Status area

The Launcher

On the left of the **Shelf** is the **Launcher button**, shown here on the right and on page 25. This is used to open the Google Search bar shown below.

Alternatively the **Launcher key** or **Search key** shown on the right and on the keyboard on page 18 has the same function as the **Launcher button**.

ALL APPS button

The Google Search Bar shown above allows you to enter *keywords* to find information on any subject. Alternatively enter a *Web address* or *URL (Uniform Resource Locator)* such as **www.babanibooks.com** to open a website.

The line of apps above, immediately below the Search Bar (starting with **Get Help**, etc.) appears automatically and shows your *recently-used* apps.

Tap the button shown on the right and above to open the **ALL APPS** screen shown on the next page.

The All Apps Screen

ALL APPS screen

Web-based Apps

When you set up a new Google Account, icons for a large number of apps are pre-installed, as shown above. As stated elsewhere, many of these icons are only *links* to launch apps or programs which are actually stored and executed on Web servers in the Clouds. So if you click one of these icons when you are *offline*, i.e. not connected to the Internet, instead of running the app the following message appears.

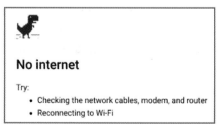

You can add more apps by downloading them from the Play Store and the Web Store, as discussed shortly. The **All Apps** display will then occupy two screens. Switch between the two **All Apps** screens by clicking one of the two buttons circled in red shown on the right and on page 27. Or use the scroll wheel on a mouse.

Default Apps

The **Shelf** shown in part below and on page 25 gives a quick way to launch apps.

When you set up a new Google Account, icons for four popular apps are *pinned* to the **Shelf** by default, as shown below. Reading from left to right, these are the Chrome Web browser, Google Mail (or Gmail) email, the Google Docs word processor and the YouTube video sharing website.

Default or pre-installed apps

Pinned Apps

Apps can be launched by clicking the **Launcher** button, then selecting the **ALL APPS** screen, as discussed on page 26, before finally clicking the icon for the required app.

To save time, icons for your *frequently-used* apps can be pinned to the **Shelf**, as discussed in Chapter 4.

The Status Area

This is the group of icons as shown below and on page 25 in their position on the extreme right of the **Shelf** .

The three icons on the **Status area,** to the left of the current time, as shown above, change to display information which varies with time, as shown in the examples below.

Number of **Notifications** or messages from Chrome OS, as discussed shortly.

Strength of Wi-Fi Internet signal. (Weak in this example because the Chromebook was quite a distance from the router.)

No Internet connection, Wi-Fi Off.

Battery fully charged

Battery currently on charge, indicated by the *lightning strike* icon.

Status Area Settings

Click anywhere on the **Status area**, shown again on the right, to display the menu panel of settings and controls shown below.

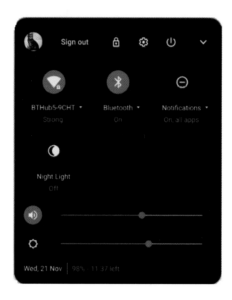

The above icons are used as follows:

This shows your *profile photo*. You can change your photo, as discussed in Chapter 4. Click the photo to see your Google Account name or sign in another user.

Require an existing user of the Chromebook to sign in with their password. **Sign out** changes to **Exit Guest** when **Browse as Guest** is switched on as discussed on pages 62 and 63.

Close the current screen and go to your **Lock Screen**, requiring your password to continue.

 Open the main **Settings** screen, discussed later in this book.

 Switch the power off, **Shut down** the Chromebook.

 Collapse the full menu panel shown on page 30.

 Expand the menu panel.

 This gives the name of your network and the signal strength. Click to switch Wi-Fi On or Off or to select another network from a list of networks within range.
Padlock icon indicates a *secure network*.

 Switch **Bluetooth** On or Off by clicking the icon. **Bluetooth** (discussed on page 114**)** is a technology for connecting devices such as computers, smartphones, tablets and headsets wirelessly over short distances.

 Notifications are messages from the Chrome OS operating system informing you of events such as an app having been upgraded or a USB device connected. Click to switch **Notifications** On or Off on selected apps.

Switch **Night Light On** or **Off**. Designed to limit bright blue light on your screen late at night and help you sleep better.

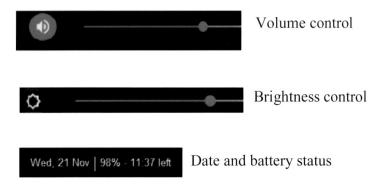

Volume control

Brightness control

Date and battery status

Switching the Chromebook On and Off

- As discussed on page 18 you can use the keyboard **Power key** to switch the Chromebook On or Off.

- Or use the **Shut down** button shown on pages 30 and 31.

- If you open the lid (i.e. screen) while the Chromebook is switched off, the Chromebook will power up and require you to sign in to your Google Account.

Sleep Mode

- If you close the lid while signed into your Google Account, the Chromebook goes into *sleep mode*. Next time you open the lid, the Chromebook returns to where it left off before the lid was closed.

Personalising Your Chromebook

Introduction

This chapter shows how you can customize a Chromebook to suit your own preferences. Changes you can make include:

- Changing the background or **wallpaper** on the *Desktop*, i.e. the Home Screen or main user interface, with icons for launching apps and menus, etc.

- *Pinning* icons for frequently used apps to the **Shelf** across the bottom of the screen to give rapid access.

- Removing from the **Shelf**, icons for apps which are no longer frequently used.

- Selecting and installing new apps from the Google Play Store.

- Selecting and installing apps, *themes*, *extensions* and games from the Chrome Web Store.

- Changing your *profile picture*.

- Checking your version of Chrome OS and updating, if necessary, to enable the Chromebook to install and run apps selected from the millions in the Google Play Store.

Changing the Desktop Wallpaper

The default background or **wallpaper** provided on a new Chromebook is shown below. As discussed below, a large number of alternative backgrounds are provided.

- Right-click anywhere on the screen as shown above, then select **Set wallpaper** as shown below.

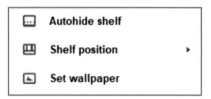

- Scroll through and browse the available samples of photos and artwork.

- Click to select your new **wallpaper**. You can also use one of your own photos as the background **wallpaper**.

Please Note:

The above **wallpaper** is the background to the main Desktop or Home Screen and not to be confused with the wallpaper on the Chrome browser, discussed on page 44.

Pinning Apps to the Shelf

When you first start using a Chromebook, a number of apps already have icons pre-installed on the **Shelf**, as shown below.

If there are apps in **ALL APPS** that you use regularly, you can save time by pinning copies of their icons to the **Shelf**.

For example, if you use **Google Photos** a lot, you would normally have to click the **Launcher** to open the **ALL APPS** screen and then click the **Photos** icon shown on the right. So you can save time by pinning the **Photos** icon to the **Shelf** as shown below and on the next page.

Photos

- Open the **ALL APPS** screen as discussed on page 26.
- Move the cursor over the **Photos** icon and right-click.
- Click **Pin to shelf** from the menu which appears, as shown below.

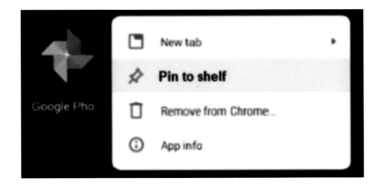

- A *copy* of the **Photos** icon is added to the **Shelf**, as shown below on the right. The original copy of the **Photos** icon remains on the **ALL APPS** screen.

Photos app
pinned to **Shelf**
by the user

Removing a Pinned App from the Shelf

- To remove an app from the **Shelf**, right-click the icon and select **Unpin** from the pop-up menu.

Apps Currently Running in a Chromebook

After you tap an icon on the **ALL APPS** screen to start running an app, the icon appears *temporarily* on the **Shelf**, as shown by the two right-hand apps below.

Default apps   Pinned app   Apps currently running

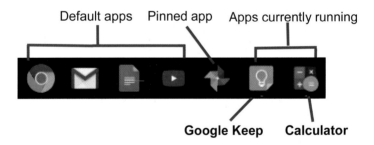

Google Keep   Calculator

- To *permanently save* or pin on the **Shelf** an app which is currently running, right-click the icon on the **Shelf** and select **Pin** from the pop-up menu.

- To close a running app and remove its icon from the **Shelf**, right-click the icon on the **Shelf** and select **Close** from the pop-up menu.

Apps Pre-installed on a Chromebook

Some very useful apps which can be launched immediately either from the **Shelf** or from the **ALL APPS** screen on a new Chromebook include:

Docs

A word processor for creating documents and reports, etc. Similar to Microsoft Word.

Sheets

A spreadsheet program for calculations on tables of figures, and producing graphs, etc.

Slides

An app or program for preparing presentations with charts, pictures, graphs and videos to show to an audience.

Gmail

A popular email program.

Hangouts

An app for making video calls, similar to Skype.

Google Keep

Make notes, reminders including lists and images, etc.

Play Music

Listen to your favourite music, make playlists, etc.

Play Movies and TV

Download and watch videos and TV shows.

Installing Additional Apps

The pre-installed apps listed on page 37 cover many of the main computing activities, whether you're using a Chromebook for your work, education or entertainment. However, for more specialised purposes there are literally millions of apps available, many of them free, in the *Google Play Store* and the *Chrome Web Store*. While many of these are games, there are also many practical apps like online banking, flight simulators and flight tracking apps. Also there are versions of the leading Microsoft Word, Excel and PowerPoint business software.

Originally Chromebooks used the Web Store as their main source of additional apps and *extensions*. Extensions are small programs giving extra functions to Chrome, the Web browser which is the main Chromebook user interface.

In recent years users of Android smartphones and tablets have had access to millions of apps in the Google Play Store. Androids and Chromebooks are both Google products and Chromebooks now also have access to the Play Store. The Play Store icon is pre-installed on the **ALL APPS** screen on new Chromebooks, as shown in the extract below.

Please note:

Some early Chromebooks can't run the Play Store apps. It may be possible to update the Chrome OS to enable the Play Store apps to be run as discussed on page 46.

Installing an App from the Play Store

- Click the **Play Store** app on the **Launcher** or **ALL APPS** screen to display the **HOME** screen shown below.

- Enter the name of an app you wish to search for, or select a **Category** you wish to browse through.

- For example, type **flight simulator** in the Search Bar shown above. Click any apps in the results which interest you and read their descriptions, price if applicable, users' reviews, etc.

In-app purchases   **READ MORE**

- When you've chosen an app, click **INSTALL** shown on the previous page to download and install the app and then click **Open** or **Launch** to start using the app.

- After you've installed apps or extensions, etc., from the Play Store (and the Web Store), their icons appear on the second **ALL APPS** screen.

- To view the new apps, scroll the screen upwards or click one of the two dots shown on the right, and on pages 27 and 28.

- These new apps can each be launched by clicking their icons on the **ALL APPS** screen.

- Alternatively, to be able to launch an app from the **Shelf** instead of the **ALL APPS** screen, right-click the icon and select **Pin to shelf** as shown on page 35.

Offline Apps

The Chromebook primarily uses the Chrome browser to run Web-based programs on the Internet. However, some programs or apps can be downloaded and run *offline*, i.e. not on the Internet in the Chrome browser. These include the **Flywings** app shown on page 39 and on the right and also above in the extract from the **ALL APPS** screen.

In-app Purchases

Some apps, initially free, offer extra features such as progressing to higher levels in a game. These can result in some large and unexpected bills, especially if young children have access to your payment facilities.

The Chrome Web Store

- Click the icon for the Web Store in the **ALL APPS** screen and shown on the right. The Web Store is displayed in the Chrome browser, as shown below.

- There are various categories of software available in the Web Store. As well as **Apps** and **Games**, there are **Extensions** and **Themes**, as shown below and discussed shortly.

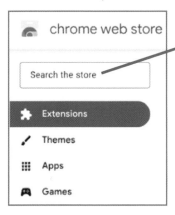

Enter keywords in the Search Bar to search through the Web Store in the categories as shown on the left. Or browse by pressing and dragging with two fingers on the touchpad or turning the scroll wheel on a mouse.

Installing an App from the Web Store

For example, suppose you want to find a drawing app for the Chromebook.

- Click the icon for the Web Store, shown on the right, on the **Launcher** or **ALL APPS** screen.

- Select **Apps**, as shown on page 41, type **drawing** in the Search Bar and press the **Enter** key.

- A list of apps matching your search criteria is displayed, including the example shown below.

- Select **Add to Chrome** shown above, followed by **Add app** to install the app, **Draw Canvas** in this example, to your **ALL APPS** screen, as shown on the right. Click the icon to start using the app.

Offline Apps in the Web Store

As mentioned elsewhere, the Chromebook is primarily designed to work with *online* apps executed on the Internet via the Chrome Web browser. However there are some apps in the Web Store that can run *offline*. These can be found by clicking in the box next to **Runs Offline** in the left-hand panel of the Web Store, as shown on the right, and on page 41 and then starting a search.

Features	
▣	Runs Offline
☐	By Google

Extensions and Themes

The method of installing **Extensions**, **Themes** and **Games** as listed on page 41 is broadly the same as installing **Apps** from the Chrome Web Store, as discussed on page 42.

Extensions

These are small programs which add extra functions to the Chrome browser, as shown in the sample below from the Chrome Web Store.

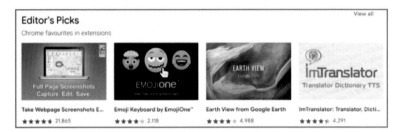

Extensions provide a wide range of extra tools to be used with Chrome, including calendars, a human–sounding reader of Web text, a dictionary and a screen capture tool.

Installed extensions appear as icons on the top right-hand corner of the Chrome browser screen, shown outlined in red below. To run an extension, click its icon.

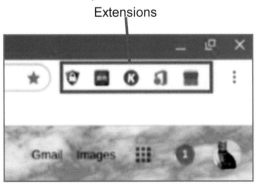

Themes

These allow you to select a different background to use with the Chrome browser.

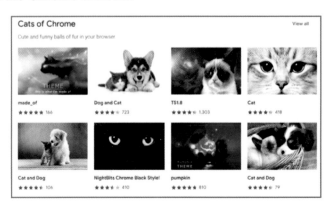

- Click to select a theme and then click **Add to Chrome**.

- The new background will appear next time you click the icon shown on the right to launch the Chrome browser.

Your Profile Picture

- Profile pictures are used on the Chromebook sign-in screen and they also appear as a form of identification on emails you send.

- If you set up a new Chromebook using an existing gmail account from a previous computer, your profile picture will be *synced* to the new machine.

- Your profile picture appears at the top right of the Chrome browser, shown on the right below.

- When you set up a new account, you can use a photo or image, as shown at the bottom of this page, or the initial of your first name is used by default.

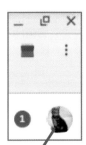

Profile picture

Changing Your Profile Picture

- Click anywhere in the **Status area** discussed on page 30 and then click the **Settings** button shown on the right.

- Click your name on the **Settings** screen.

- Take a photo using the Chromebook Webcam, or browse for a photo on your Chromebook or select one of the many images provided, as shown below.

Use the webcam   Browse folders   Select image

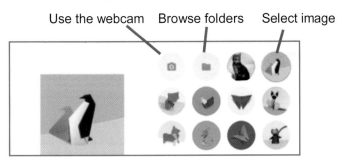

Updating Chrome OS

As stated on page 38, the latest Chromebooks have access to millions of apps in the Google Play Store. To use these apps you need version 53 of the Chrome OS or later.

- Click anywhere in the **Status area** and then click the **Settings** button shown on the right. Scroll down the **Settings** to the **Google Play Store** section.

- You should see **Install apps and games from Google Play on Your Chromebook** as shown below.

If you don't see the above statement, you may not be able to use the Play Store apps. Check your version of Chrome OS as follows:

- Click the **Settings** menu button shown on the right, at the top left of the main **Settings** screen.

- Click **About Chrome OS** at the bottom of the menu.

- This displays the version number of your Chrome OS such as the current latest **Version 70.....** shown below.

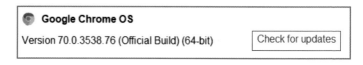

- Select **Check for updates**, shown above on the right. Chrome OS will install any available updates.

The Chrome Browser

Introduction

Google Chrome, or simply Chrome, is the world's leading *Web browser*. It's not to be confused with *Chrome OS*, the *operating system* which takes care of all the basic functions needed to run the Chromebook computer.

Chrome is at the heart of the Chromebook and provides the *user interface* for most of your activities, such as:

- To search for and display information after typing or speaking *keywords* into the search bar.

- To access Web pages after entering an *address*, such as **www.babanibooks.com**, into the browser.

- To move between Web pages by tapping *links* or *hyperlinks* on a Web page and move forwards and backwards between Web pages.

- To use *tabs* to switch between open Web pages.

- To *bookmark* Web pages for revisiting later.

- To launch and run *Web-based* apps or programs on the Internet.

- To display the results of running a program.

- To run *extensions* or *plug-ins* which add extra functions to Chrome.

Searching with Google

Google is the world's leading *search engine*. It is so widely used that the verb *to Google* means to search the Internet for information. The search engine scans millions of Web pages to find those that match your search criteria. It then displays the results as a list of clickable links to those Web pages containing the information you're looking for.

The Keyword Search

The *Google Search Bar* is used to enter the keywords relating to the information you are interested in. The Search Bar is displayed on several different Chrome screens. The quickest way to display the Search Bar is to press the **Search** or **Launcher** key or click the **Launcher** button on the left of the **Shelf**, shown below and on pages 25 and 26.

Launcher button   Search or Launcher key

The launcher screen opens, displaying the Search Bar as shown below.

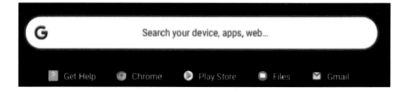

Enter the keyword(s) you wish to search for into the Search Bar, such as **alpaca** shown on the next page, and then press **Enter**.

A long list of results containing the word **alpaca** is then displayed in Chrome, as shown in the small extract below.

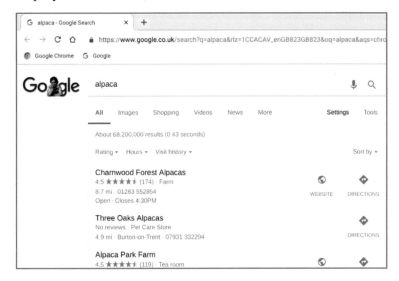

Each result above is a clickable link to a website, as shown below, containing information on your chosen subject.

The Voice Search

When the Chrome browser opens as shown at the top of page 49, the Google Search Bar is again displayed.

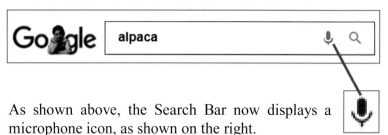

As shown above, the Search Bar now displays a microphone icon, as shown on the right.

The microphone on the Chromebook is located near the centre of the *bezel* or frame at the top of the screen, as shown on page 14.

- Click the microphone icon shown above.
- The screen displays **Speak now** and then **Listening**....
- Speak the keyword(s) clearly towards the microphone.
- The list of search results should appear, as shown on page 49.

Searching for a Website Address

Every website has a unique address, known as its *URL*, or *Uniform Resource Locator*. A typical Web address is :

www.babanibooks.com

As indicated below, instead of a keyword search you can enter a URL into the Google Search Bar.

- Type the address or URL into the search bar as shown on the previous page and press **Enter** or **Return**.

- This opens the website, such as **www.rspb.org.uk**, shown in the Chrome browser below.

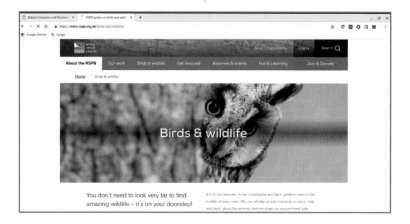

Searching within Google Chrome

In the previous examples, the Google Search Bar was displayed quickly by using the **Launcher** button on the **Shelf** or the **Launcher** or **Search** key on the keyboard.

The Search Bar can also be displayed within Google Chrome as shown on the next page.

To launch Google Chrome, tap its icon, shown on the right, on the **ALL APPS** screen or on the **Shelf**, shown below and discussed on page 25.

The Chrome Home Page opens, as shown below.

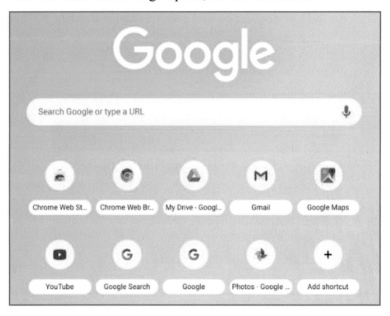

At the centre of the Chrome screen is the Google Search bar shown above. This can be used to search for websites using keywords or URLs as discussed on the previous pages.

Also shown above are the icons giving quick access or *shortcuts* to many of the Chromebook's own apps such as Gmail and Photos. These all operate as websites in the Chrome browser and you can add more after clicking **Add shortcut**, shown above. Then enter the **Name** and **URL** of the website.

Searching for Anything

The Web is surely the world's largest and most up-to-date encyclopaedia covering almost every known subject, no matter how bizarre. For example, type any task, such as **grooming a dog that bites** and numerous Web sites offer helpful advice, including step-by-step videos.

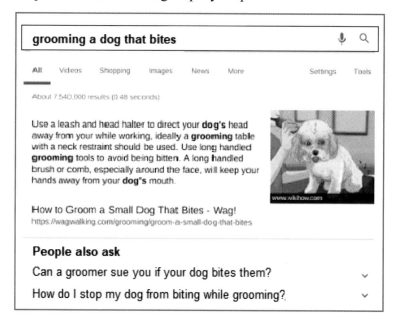

Try typing a few diverse keywords into Google Chrome and see how easy it is to find good information on virtually any subject. Here's a few random examples to get you started:

mending a puncture	electric car	bluetooth
shearing a sheep	capability brown	growing orchids
meerkat	halebop	cpu

Links to Other Web Pages

Move the cursor around a Web page such as the RSPB example on page 51, by moving the mouse or by sliding a finger across the touchpad. As the cursor passes over certain screen objects such as words or icons, etc., it changes from an arrowhead to a hand. This means the cursor is over a *link* or *hyperlink*. Click the link to display another Web page, perhaps on the same or another website.

At the top left-hand corner of the Chrome screen there are icons, shown highlighted in red below, to help you move *forward* and *back* between the Web pages you've visited as you *browsed* or *surfed* the Internet.

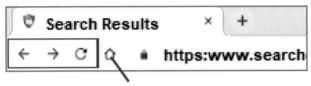

Open Chrome Home Page (shown on page 52)

As shown on page 18, the Chromebook keyboard has special function keys along the top to help with browsing, as follows:

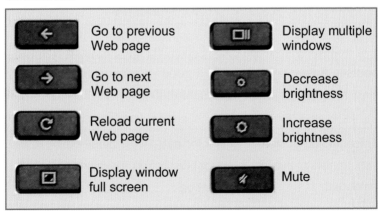

Tabbed Browsing

When you launch the Chrome browser as discussed on page 51, the top left-hand corner displays **New Tab** as shown below. This is similar to a paper tab used to divide a ring binder into sections. A tab allows many Web pages to be displayed in a single window.

- If you now start a search by entering a keyword such as **birds** in the Search Bar and pressing **Enter**, the keyword(s) appear on the tab, as shown below.

- Now start browsing by clicking the link on one of the search results and then clicking further links to browse around different Web pages on a website.

- As you move to different Web pages, the title of each new page replaces the title of the previous page on the tab.

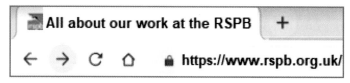

- As discussed on page 54, use the forward and back buttons on the screen or the keys on the keyboard.

Opening a New Tab

If you start a new search by entering a keyword in the Search Bar, the new search and any pages you browse to will be accessible on the tab shown on the previous page.

However, you may wish to keep your browsing on the new keyword separate from the previous subject. This can easily be done by clicking the + sign shown below to open a new tab.

New tab

So you can have several tabs on the screen at the same time, each giving access to a large number of Web pages. Click to select a tab then move between the various Web pages using the forward and back buttons on the screen or on the Chromebook keyboard.

Tabs representing different searches

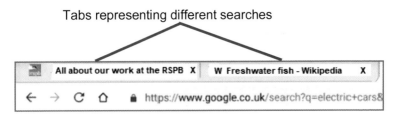

If you finish a session you can return to the tabs later by clicking the 3-dot menu button at the top right of the Chrome screen and selecting **History** from the **Customise and control Google Chrome** menu shown on the next page.

Customise and control

The Chrome Customise and Control Menu

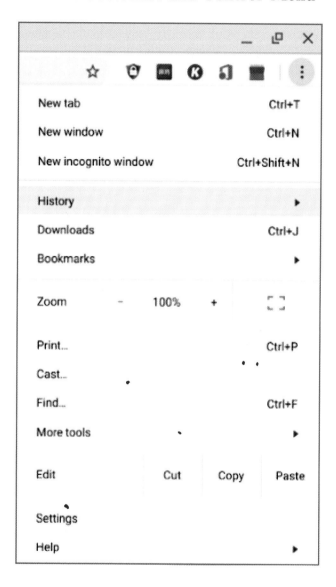

The History Menu

The **History** menu mentioned on pages 56 and 57 and shown below lists your recently visited Web pages. These can be re-opened by clicking their entry in the list.

Clearing Your Browsing History

You may wish to remove your **History** and other browsing data, perhaps to protect your privacy and also to save space on your Internal Storage.

- To remove the list of Web pages from your **History**, click **More tools** from the menu shown on page 57, then click **Clear browsing data....**
- The menu shown at the top of page 59 opens.
- Select a **Time range** from the drop-down menu.
- Select with a tick which other data to remove, as well as your **History**. Click **Clear data**.

(*Cookies* are small files which record your browsing preferences and activities. *Cached images and files* are data saved on your Internal Storage to save time downloading them again when you revisit websites).

Bookmarking a Web Page

- If you see a Web page you like and may wish to revisit in the future, click the star icon near the top right of the Chrome screen.

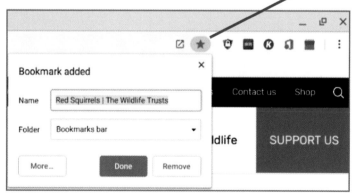

- The **Bookmark** window opens, as shown on the previous page. Accept the name for the bookmark suggested by Chrome or enter another name.

- Similarly you can accept the default **Folder**, i.e. the **Bookmarks bar** shown below, or select another **Folder** from the drop-down menu.

- Click **Done** shown at the bottom of page 59 to include the **Red Squirrels** Web page on the **Bookmarks bar** near the top of the Chrome screen as shown below.

- At any future time, click the bookmark to re-open the Web page as shown above.

- You can **Delete** a bookmark after right-clicking it in the **Bookmarks bar**. Or select **Bookmarks** on the menu shown on page 57 and right-click the bookmark, then click **Delete**.

Incognito Browsing

When you browse the Internet you leave a trail of information which other people may be able to see. Some of this information may be personal and you may prefer to keep it confidential. This browsing information includes the **History** of Web sites you've visited and *cookies* or small text files recording your browsing habits.

Some people regard the collection of browsing data using cookies, often used to target you with advertising, as an invasion of privacy. As discussed on pages 58 and 59, you can clear your browsing data, but you need to remember to do it regularly.

Also you may not wish a close friend or relative to know what websites you've been looking at, especially if you've been secretly researching the symptoms of a serious illness, for example. *Incognito Browsing*, also known as *Private Browsing*, does not save your browsing **History** or cookies.

- To start **Incognito browsing**, open the main **Customise and control** menu, as discussed on pages 56 and 57.

- Select **New incognito window**.

- The following explanatory window appears on a new tab, as shown below.

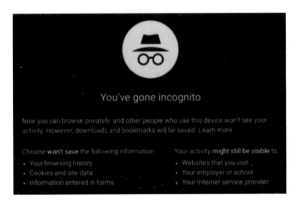

You've gone incognito

Now you can browse privately, and other people who use this device won't see your activity. However, downloads and bookmarks will be saved. Learn more

Chrome won't save the following information: Your activity might still be visible to:
- Your browsing history   - Websites that you visit
- Cookies and site data   - Your employer or school
- Information entered in forms   - Your Internet service provider

- Start browsing after entering a keyword or URL in the Search Bar or by clicking a Web page in the Bookmarks bar discussed on page 60.
- During **Incognito browsing** each Web page you visit displays the *spectacles icon*, shown on the left below, near the top right-hand corner of the screen.

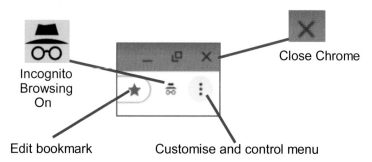

Incognito
Browsing
On

Close Chrome

Edit bookmark

Customise and control menu

- To finish **Incognito browsing**, click the cross at the top right-hand corner of the screen, as shown above on the right.

Browsing as a Guest

This option is useful if you want to let someone else use your computer or you want to borrow someone else's computer.

- When browsing as a **Guest** your **History** and cookies won't be saved after you sign out.
- Files you download and bookmarks you create will not be saved.
- The **Guest** user can't see the browsing history of the main user of the Chromebook.
- When browsing as a **Gues**t you gain some privacy but employers and network managers in schools, colleges, offices, etc., may still be able to see what you've been doing.

Turning On Browsing as a Guest

- Click anywhere on the **Status area** shown on the right, at the bottom right of the screen.

- Click **Sign out** shown   below and at the top of the **Status area** menu panel shown on page 30.

- The **Sign in** screen opens as shown below.

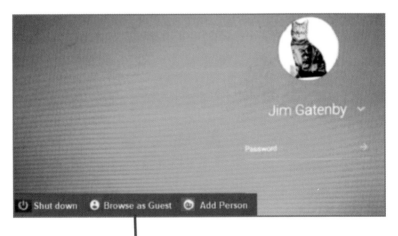

- Click **Browse as Guest** shown above to start.

Turning Off Browsing as a Guest

- Click anywhere on the **Status area** and then click **Exit guest**, shown below, which replaces the normal **Sign out** option, shown above, when you are browsing in **Guest** mode.

Multi-tasking

Much of the time when using a computer, we might only have one window open, occupying the whole screen. However, it's easy to set up multiple windows for different tasks and switch between them. Or you might want to display two windows on the screen at the same time to compare them or move data between them.

Opening Multiple Windows

If you are browsing in a window in Chrome you can easily open further windows as follows:

- Click the **Customise and control** icon shown on the right, at the top right of the screen.

- Then click **New window** from the **Customise and control** menu, shown in part below and on page 57.

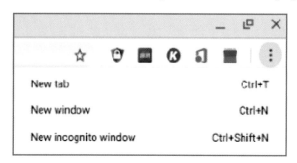

- Open the next Web page you want to view by searching with a keyword or entering a URL.

- Continue clicking **New window** and selecting any further Web pages you want to look at.

- To see all of the windows on the screen at the same time as shown on the next page, click the Chromebook function key shown on the right and on pages 18 and 54.

If you have a lot of windows open you can scroll them across the screen to select the one you want to use, as follows:

- Hold down the **alt** key and press the **tab** key.
- The windows are scrolled across the screen.
- Each of the windows is highlighted in turn.
- Release the **alt** key to open the highlighted window.

If necessary, to view the window full screen, click the **Maximise** icon at the top right-hand corner of the screen, shown below.

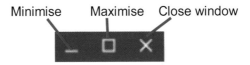

Instead of the **Maximise** icon shown above, you may see the **Restore** icon shown below. This restores a window to its previous size. Click this icon to display the **Maximise** icon shown above.

The **Maximise** icon enlarges a window, usually to fill the whole screen.

The **Minimise** icon shown above hides the window, but keeps the Web page or app open in the background.

Opening Two Windows Side by Side

On the first window click and hold the **Maximise** icon shown on the right and on page 65 and drag the window to the left or right, then release when it's in position. Repeat for the second window to display both windows side by side, as shown below.

Maximise

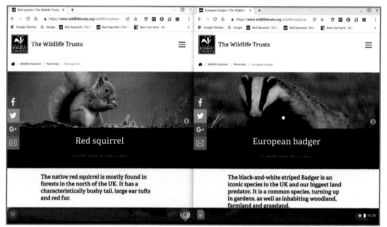

Two windows running side by side on the screen

Chrome: More than a Web Browser

Google Chrome is the leading Web browser, used for retrieving Web pages from the Internet. However, as mentioned elsewhere, Chrome has another role in the Chromebook. Chrome provides the user interface and the windows in which Web-based programs are displayed.

So programs such as the **Docs** word processor and the **Sheets** spreadsheet can be run side by side on the screen as discussed above. Then, for example, you could copy data from a spreadsheet and include it in a document in the word processor.

6

Starting Work

Introduction

As mentioned earlier, the Chromebook has access to many thousands of apps, some of them pre-installed or available from the Play Store or the Web Store.

While many of these apps are games or entertainment, there is also some extremely useful software for more productive work. This software will be particularly useful, for example, if you are a student in school or college, working in an office or small business or writing your first novel or autobiography.

Productive software includes the following Google apps:

Docs
A fully featured word processor for writing letters, reports, coursework projects, etc.

Sheets
A powerful spreadsheet for calculations on tables of figures and for easily drawing graphs and charts.

Slides
A program for preparing presentations to an audience, including notes, images and graphs.

Keep
An app for saving notes in the form of text, lists, images and voice recordings.

Google Docs, Sheets and Slides above are free with the Chromebook and perform similar functions to the relatively expensive Microsoft Word, Excel and PowerPoint, with which they can exchange files.

Word Processing with Google Docs

- Launch **Docs** by clicking its icon on the **All Apps** screen or on the **Shelf**.

- **Google Docs** opens in its own tab in the Chrome Browser, as shown below.

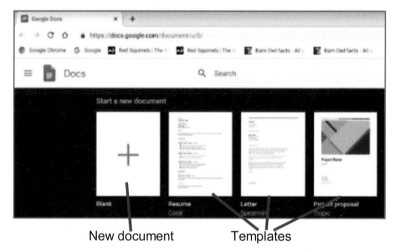

New document   Templates

- The opening **Docs** screen above is running in the Chrome browser and displaying the Web pages in your **Bookmarks bar** and forward and back buttons.

- On the right above are 3 samples of the range of *templates* provided, allowing you to base your new document on a previously-designed format.

- Also displayed on the opening screen are thumbnails for your recent documents. Click one of these thumbnails to re-open and continue working on a document.

- Click the **Blank** thumbnail shown above to open a new **Untitled document**, as shown in the extract on page 69.

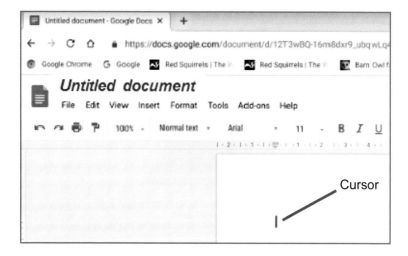

- The blank screen is ready for you to start typing at the flashing cursor, as shown above.

- If you don't see **Untitled document**, shown above, click the arrow near the top right of the screen. This switches on or off the menu bar starting **File**, **Edit**, **View**, etc., shown above.

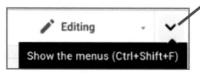

- To give your document a name, click *Untitled document* shown above and replace it with your own name such as **Chromebook** shown below.

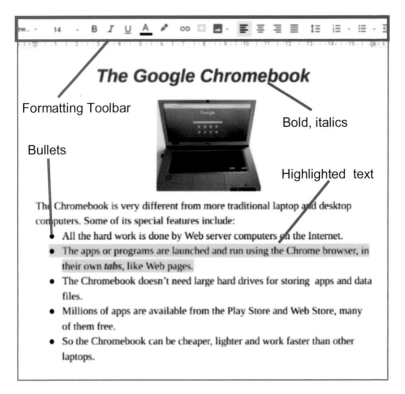

Google Docs, used to create the document shown above, is supplied free with the Chromebook. **Docs** has many of the features of the world's leading word processing software, Microsoft Word, with which it is highly compatible. These features include:

- Text formats such as *bold* and *italic* with different *fonts*, i.e. styles and sizes of lettering.

- Alignment of text, *centred*, *left* and *right justified*, and *fully justified*.

- Arranging text in lists using *bullets* and *numbering*.

- Inserting and positioning *images*, *photographs*, etc.

Highlighting or Selecting Text

Before you can change the format of an existing piece of text, you need to *highlight* or *select* it, as shown in yellow on the previous page. To highlight a piece of text:

- With the cursor at the beginning of the text to be highlighted, press and hold the touchpad with one finger. Then slide with a second finger over all the text to be highlighted.

- Alternatively, with a mouse, click and hold then drag the cursor over the text to be highlighted.

- Select a highlighting colour, as shown on page 73.

- To remove the highlighting, click with the cursor positioned outside of the highlighted area.

Toolbar Icons

Highlight the text to be changed then select the required icons from the Toolbar, shown outlined in red at the top of page 70. These are listed below and on the next few pages, working from left to right across the Toolbar.

Undo   Cancel the previous action. Useful if you make a mistake.

Redo   Repeat the action just cancelled.

Print   Print on paper one or more copies of a document such as a report, project, etc.

The next section of the Toolbar is shown below.

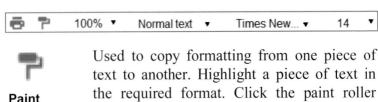

Paint format

Used to copy formatting from one piece of text to another. Highlight a piece of text in the required format. Click the paint roller shown on the left then click and drag the cursor over the text to be formatted.

| Zoom | Click the down arrow then select a smaller or larger display size of the document on the screen. |

Zoom

Click the down arrow then select a smaller or larger display size of the document on the screen.

Styles

Click the down arrow to select from various styles for headings and titles, etc.

Fonts

Click the down arrow to select from various fonts or styles of lettering such as **Times New Roman** shown on the left.

Font size

Click the down arrow next to **14** in this example, to choose the size of lettering measured in *points* or *pts*. Font sizes in **Docs** range from 8pts to 96pts.

Font effects

Click these icons, also shown on the Toolbar on page 73, to apply **Bold**, **Italic** and **Underline** or any combination of these effects to a highlighted piece of text.

Text colour

Highlight a piece of text, then click this icon, also shown on the Toolbar above, to select the *font colour* for the highlighted text, as shown in the small sample below.

Highlight colour

Click this icon, also shown on the Toolbar above, to change the *highlighting* colour. This is the background colour, shown in yellow on page 70, unlike the **Text colour** discussed above.

Link

Insert into a document a clickable link to a Web site, after entering the name to appear on the document and then pasting a link or searching for the Web address.

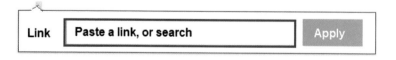

Comment

Highlight a piece of text and write some comments about it. Include a person's email address to get their response.

The final group of icons on the right of the Toolbar is shown below.

Image

Click this icon, also shown on the Toolbar above, to insert an image from the sources shown in the menu which appears. These sources include your computer, the Web, the Drive folder, your Photos folder and the Chromebook Camera.

Text alignment

These icons on the Toolbar, also shown above, are used to control the *justification* i.e. *vertical alignment in a straight line* of a highlighted piece of text.

Reading from left to right, these are *left justified*, *centred*, *right justified* and *fully justified*. *Fully justified* means vertically aligned on both the left-hand and right-hand sides of the text.

Listed below and on page 75 are the six icons on the right of the formatting Toolbar shown at the top of this page.

Line spacing

Set the spacing in **pts** between lines of text and before and after paragraphs

Numbered list

Number the items in a list, with several number formats to choose from.

Add a bullet point to emphasis each separate statement in a list.

Bulleted list

Decrease the number of spaces at the left of a selected block of text.

Decrease indent

Increase the number of spaces at the left of a selected block of text.

Increase indent

Remove formatting such as bold, italics, underline and text colour from selected text.

Clear formatting

The Spelling Checker

After typing a document, select **Tools** then **Spelling** from the **Files**, **Edit**, **View...** menu bar shown near the top of page 69. Then select **Spell check** shown below.

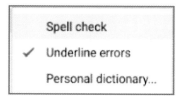

By default any spelling errors are highlighted and underlined and Docs suggests alternative spellings to insert. You can also add words to a **Personal dictionary**.

Switching Formatting On and Off as You Type

The previous section discussed applying formatting effects such as bold, italics, underline and font sizes and colours. These notes, on pages 71-75, described applying the effects to blocks of existing text on the screen, i.e. *highlighted* or *selected* words, sentences, paragraphs, etc.

However, these effects can also be switched on *before* you type the text.

- Simply switch On the effect such as *italics* by clicking the italics icon on the Toolbar shown at the bottom of page 72.

- Switch Off the formatting effect, such as italics, by clicking the Toolbar icon again.

- The formatting icons act as *toggles*, i.e. used to alternately switch effects On then Off.

Capital Letters

- The Chromebook doesn't have the **Caps Lock** key usually present on the left-hand side of a keyboard.

- Instead the Chromebook uses **alt+search** (hold down the **alt** key and press the **search** key) to switch capitals On and Off.

  Search key

Keyboard Shortcuts

The combination of key presses **alt+search** shown above is an example of a *keyboard shortcut* as discussed on page 79. Many of these are standard on computer systems in general, not just the Chromebook.

Cut and Paste

This is used to *move* a piece of text, such as a word, a paragraph or a page, to a new location, in the same document or in a different document.

- Select the text to be moved as discussed on page 71.
- Right-click over the selected text and click **Cut** from the menu which appears.

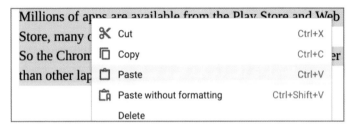

- The selected text is deleted from its original location and saved on the *clipboard,* a temporary store in the memory of the Chromebook.
- Place the cursor at the start of the new position for the text then right-click and select **Paste** from the menu, to place the text in its new location.

Copy and Paste

If you select **Copy**, instead of **Cut** as shown on the menu above, the selected text remains in its original position and a *duplicate copy* is placed in the new location in the document when you right-click and select **Paste**.

Please note on the above menu:

- **Delete** completely removes the selected text.
- Instead of clicking the menu options you can use keyboard shortcuts such as **Ctrl+X**, **Ctrl+C** and **Ctrl+V**. (More keyboard shortcuts are listed on page 79).

Inserting an Image into a Document

- Type the text of the document.
- Insert the cursor approximately where you want the image to appear.
- Select the **Image** icon shown on the right.
- Next select the source of your image from the menu which appears, such as **Google Drive**, your **Photos** folder or the Chromebook **Camera**.
- Select the image or photo to use and then click **Insert**.

Meadow

Meadow is a rescue cat, found abandoned in a field. At first she was very frightened and remained hidden for days. Gradually she has gained confidence and is becoming quite arrogant.

However, as long as her food is served on time, she treats us quite well and is a good employer.

- Click over the image to display the options shown below, to align the text relative to the image.

In line | Wrap text | Break text

- Click and drag the image to its final position.
- Right-click the image to display a menu including the option to **Crop** the image.
- To *resize* the image, select it and drag one of the small squares which appear around the image frame.

Keyboard Shortcuts

Some operations can be carried out more quickly using keyboard shortcuts, as mentioned on pages 76 and 77, rather than searching through menus. Shortcuts usually involve holding down a key such as **ctrl** and pressing one or two more keys. So, for example, **ctrl+a** means "while holding down the key marked **ctrl**, press the **a** key".

The Chromebook has a very long list of shortcuts. A few examples are shown below:

- Select or highlight everything on a page   **ctrl+a**

- Copy selected text to the *clipboard*   **ctrl+c**

- Cut selected text to the clipboard   **ctrl+x**

- Paste text from the clipboard   **ctrl+v**

- Print the current page   **ctrl+p**

- Undo your last action   **ctrl+z**

- Redo your last action   **shift+ctrl+z**

- Open a new window as shown on page 52   **ctrl+n**

- Open a new tab, as shown on page 56   **ctrl+t**
- Add **www.** and .com to the text in the   **ctrl+enter**
  address bar then open the Web page

- Show all keyboard shortcuts   **ctrl+alt+/**

Please note, on some keyboards the keys are labelled as **ctrl**, **shift** and **c** for example, while others use **Ctrl**, **Shift** and **C**.

Saving a Document

- When you type a document in Google Docs, it's saved automatically.

- When you edit a document these changes are also saved automatically.

- By default a new document is saved with the file name, ***Untitled document*** as shown on page 69.

- To save the document with a more meaningful *file name*, delete ***Untitled document*** and replace with your own file name, such as ***Latest News*** shown below.

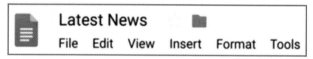

- Your documents are automatically saved in the **My Drive** folder on the Internet, not on the local Internal Storage on your Chromebook. So they are available to you on *any computer*, *anywhere in the world*.

- However, to access files in **My Drive** you must be connected to the Internet and signed in to your Google Account, as discussed on page 23.

Managing Files

The **Files** app, discussed in Chapter 8, is used to:

- Manage, as *files*, documents or output produced in Docs, Sheets and Slides mentioned on page 67.

- Copy files between your **My Drive** folder on the Internet and the **Downloads** folder on your device.

- Copy files to and from removable devices such as USB flash drives and external hard drives, etc.

Managing and printing documents and compatibility with MS Office files is also covered in Chapter 8.

Google Sheets, Slides and Keep

Introduction

Chapter 6 discussed the Google Docs word processor. This has many similar features to the best selling Microsoft Word. Word is part of Microsoft Office, along with the Excel Spreadsheet and PowerPoint presentation software.

In the same way, the Chromebook has its own free Sheets spreadsheet and Slides presentation software, similar to Microsoft Excel and PowerPoint. The Google Keep app used for note taking is also covered in this chapter.

Sheets

Slides

Keep

Chapter 6 discussed in detail the many formatting tools available in Google Docs. These are used for tasks such as changing the fonts or styles of lettering, and effects such as bold and italics and different colours for text. Also the starting and naming of a new document and the automatic saving in **My Drive**.

Many of the above formatting and other tasks discussed for Google Docs in Chapter 6 also apply to Google Sheets and Slides covered in this chapter. If necessary please refer back to Chapter 6 for help with formatting and other tasks common to Docs, Sheets and Slides.

The Google Sheets Spreadsheet

A spreadsheet takes the hard work out of lengthy, repetitive and complex calculations. Microsoft Excel is the most widely used spreadsheet program in the world but Google Sheets is a worthy alternative and supplied free, built into the Chromebook.

The spreadsheet is used to manage accounts and produce graphs and statistics in business, colleges and other organisations. Google Sheets is also very suitable for the home user wishing to keep a tight rein on their finances. In fact the spreadsheet can be used wherever calculations are required on rows or columns of figures. Shown below is a simple spreadsheet based on plant sales in a small business.

	Plant Sales ☆ ■		
	File Edit View Insert Format Data Tools Add-ons		
	100% ▾ £ % .0 .00 123 ▾ Arial		
fx	Description		
	A	B	C	D
1	Description	Unit Price	Number Sold	Sales
2		£		£
3	Lettuce	0.05	400	20.00
4	Tomatoes	0.25	60	15.00
5	Courgettes	0.04	24	0.96
6	Runner beans	0.04	180	7.20
7		Total Sales	664	43.16

As can be seen above, the Sheets spreadsheet app has many similar features to the Docs wordprocessor discussed in Chapter 6.

Sheets

- The spreadsheet is opened from its icon on the **All Apps** screen or on the **Shelf**. There are thumbnails for a new sheet, ready-made templates and recent spreadsheets, similar to the Doc files shown on page 68.

- The new spreadsheet opens with the name *Untitled spreadsheet*, as shown below. This can be replaced with your own filename, as discussed on page 69.

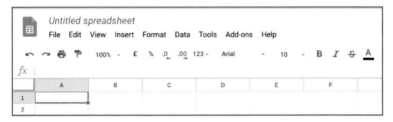

- The Toolbar has all the formatting features such as fonts, text sizes, colours and bold and italic, etc.

- There are icons for undoing and redoing actions, "painting" a format onto other text or numbers and printing a spreadsheet, as shown on the left above and on pages 71 and 72.

- The **File** tab above is used for tasks such as opening, downloading and renaming files.

- The spreadsheet consists of a table of *cells* identified by "grid references" such as **C4** and **D4** shown on page 82.

- A cell can contain text or numbers or a *formula* to carry out a calculation.

- Move around the spreadsheet by sliding a finger over the touchpad or moving a mouse.

- Tap or click in a cell to start typing numbers or letters. Press **Enter** or **Return** to move down a column after entering data into a cell.

Calculations

Simple formulas, such as multiplying two cells together, can be entered by typing into a cell, preceded by an equals sign, as in **=B3*C3** shown in cell **D3** below. (The asterisk * is generally used for multiplication in computing, while / is used for division.)   After pressing **Enter** or **Return**, the answer, **20** in this example, appears in the cell where the formula was entered.

=B3*C3

fx	=B3*C3			
	A	B	C	D
1	Description	Unit Price	Number Sold	Sales
2		£		£
3	Lettuce	0.05	400	=B3*C3
4	Tomatoes	0.25	60	15.00

For more complex calculations, select the cell where the answer is to appear. Then select the *sigma* symbol shown on the right. This appears at the extreme right of the Sheets Toolbar. Then select the mathematical function you wish to use, such as **SUM** or **AVERAGE** shown below.

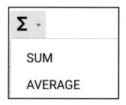

Selecting Cells

For calculations such as totalling rows or columns of figures or finding averages, first select the required cells by tapping with one finger then sliding over the required cells with another finger. Or with a mouse click and hold then drag the cursor. Then select the required mathematical function and press **Enter** or **Return.**

Selecting Rows and Columns

To select entire rows or columns, click the number at the left of a row or the letter at the top of a column. Once selected or highlighted the data in the row or column can be formatted, as discussed in Chapter 6, or deleted. To delete, press with two fingers or right-click, then select **Delete row** or **Delete column** from the menu which appears.

Number Formats

Numerical data in spreadsheets can be formatted in several different ways. For example, money in pounds will normally be displayed with two decimal places as in the **Unit Price** on page 84, while **Number Sold** is an integer or whole number. The number formats appear on the Sheets Toolbar on pages 82 and 83 and are shown again below.

£ **Currency**: Add £ sign and 2 decimal places

% Express as a %. E,g. **.50** becomes **50.00%**

.0 .00 Decrease or increase the number of decimal places

123 ▾ Open a menu displaying more number format options

Replicating a Formula

One of the great strengths of the spreadsheet is that you only have to enter a formula once at the top of a column or at the beginning of a row. Then you drag a small cross from the bottom right corner of the cell containing the formula, all the way down the column or along the row. This applies the formula to all the other cells in the row or column. A big spreadsheet could have many more rows or columns than the small example shown on page 82. This *replication* of formulas can save a great deal of work.

Recalculation

Another very important spreadsheet function is to carry out "what if?" speculations. For example:

- What if inflation reached 5%?
- What if petrol were to cost £2.00 a litre?
- What if savings interest rates were 3%, 4%, or 5%, etc.?

The spreadsheet program makes it very easy to feed in variables like these and then recalculate a very large table, perhaps containing hundreds of numbers, in seconds, helping to predict possible future scenarios.

Auto-save

As you create, make changes or edit a spreadsheet in Sheets or a document in Docs, the amended file is automatically saved in the **My Drive** folder, within **Google Drive**, as discussed in more detail in Chapter 8. This is confirmed by a note above the Sheets Toolbar, outlined in red below.

Spreadsheet Graphs and Charts

The spreadsheet program can quickly turn columns or rows of figures into graphs and charts.

- Drag to highlight or select the required rows or columns.

- Multiple columns or rows can be selected for use in the graph by holding down the **Ctrl** key.

- Select the **Insert chart** icon shown on the right and on the right of the Sheets Toolbar, shown below.

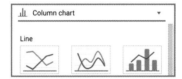

- Click the arrow to the right of **Chart type** to select the type of graph or chart you want to draw, as shown in the small sample below.

As shown in the example below, the spreadsheet program works out the scales and labels the axes automatically.

Please Note:

More information about spreadsheets can be found in BP765 "Understanding Excel Spreadsheets for Everyone" by Jim Gatenby (9780859347655).

Google Slides

Slides is similar to Microsoft PowerPoint, widely used for *presentations* or lectures to an audience. Slides can also be used for displaying family photos or to illustrate an informal talk to a club or to a group of friends. A presentation consists of several slides or separate pages and a slide can include media such as text, graphics, audio, video and animations. You can add sound such as a commentary and the slides can be moved on automatically or under the control of the touchpad or a mouse.

After clicking the **Slides** icon on the **All Apps** screen or on the **Shelf**, you are presented with an opening screen with thumbnails to **Start a new presentation** or open a ready-made template which can be edited for your own requirements.

Slides

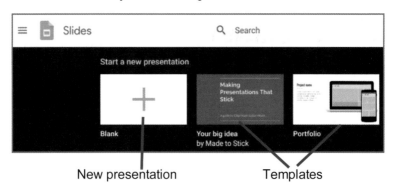

New presentation   Templates

Completed slides also appear as thumbnails on the opening screen and can be opened for editing by clicking.

As shown on the next page, the user interface in Slides is very similar to those used in Google Docs and Sheets. The Toolbar across the top of the screen is still present, with the usual icons for formatting selected text such as bold, italic, fonts and colours.

Toolbar   Themes

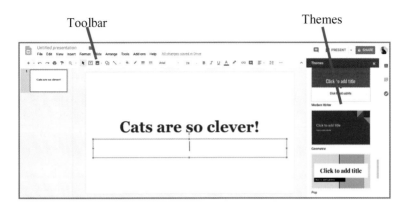

Type your titles and text in the boxes provided and in any text boxes you create. Selected text can be formatted using the Toolbar below, as discussed in Chapter 6 for Docs.

Insert

Various **Themes** as shown on the right and at the top of this page, in the right-hand panel, can be selected by clicking.

Click **Insert** shown above to add multi-media such as an image, photo, text box, video, charts and animation, shown on the right. Replace *Untitled presentation*, shown on the right, with a file name of your choice.

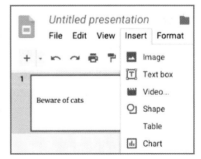

- Click **Slide** on the Toolbar, then click **New slide** from the menu, to open a blank screen for a new slide.

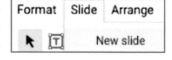

- As shown above, your completed slides are displayed as thumbnail images in the left-hand panel.

- Your presentation, i.e. set of slides, is automatically saved as a single **Google Presentation** file in your **My Drive** folder. The file size is limited to 100MB, enough for a very large number of slides.

- To start a presentation, click the play button on the left of **PRESENT** at the top right screen of the Slides screen, shown below.

- To deliver a presentation to an audience, connect the Chromebook to a monitor, as discussed in Chapter 9, using an *HDMI cable* plugged into the *HDMI port* on the Chromebook, as shown on page 13.

- To send a copy of a presentation to other people, click **SHARE** at the top right of the Slides screen and shown near the bottom of page 90.
- Enter their names or email addresses and click **Done**.

- To make your presentation viewable online, click **File** and **Publish to the web**. This provides a **Link**, i.e. a *URL* or Web address which you send to other people, allowing them to access your presentation.
- Alternatively *Embed* the presentation file in your Website to allow others to view it.

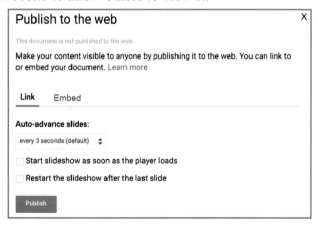

- Friends and colleagues can add comments and their name, after clicking **Insert** and **Comment**.

Google Keep

This app, supplied free with the Chromebook, is used for quickly making notes and reminders as an alternative to using scraps of paper, etc.

Keep

- Click the **Google Keep** icon on the **All Apps** screen or on the **Shelf**.

- Start typing in the **Take a note...** bar shown below.

- Icons shown on the right below allow you to create a new note as a list or include a drawing or an image.

- When you've typed the note click **Close** to display it, as shown below.

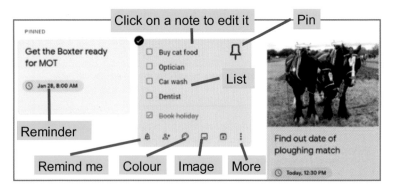

The **Pin** icon moves a top priority note to the top left of the screen. Click again to unpin the note.

Set a **Reminder** to pop up on the bottom right of the screen at a certain date and time.

Managing Your Files

Introduction

Chapters 6 and 7 discussed three important programs or apps built into the Google Drive Cloud Storage system. These are the Docs word processor, the Sheets spreadsheet and the Slides presentation app.

Docs, Sheets, and Slides produce information in different formats, i.e. text documents, tables of figures (plus graphs and charts) and slides for presentations. However, in each case the information is saved automatically as a *file*. You can give the file a meaningful name and a *filename extension* is added automatically. The filename extensions used for Google files are **.gdoc**, **.gsheet** and **.gslides**.

The Files App

The **Files** app is used to manage files in *folders* such as **My Drive** and **Downloads**, shown on the next page. The **Files** app is launched by clicking its icon, shown on the right, on the **ALL APPS** screen. Alternatively click the **Launcher** button or press the **Launcher** key, as discussed on pages 26 and 27, then click the **Files** icon.

Files

The **Files** app opens as shown below, with the **My Drive** folder selected, discussed on page 95 onwards. The other folders used to store your files outlined in red below are **Downloads**, **Offline** and **USB DISK**. These are also discussed in the rest of this chapter.

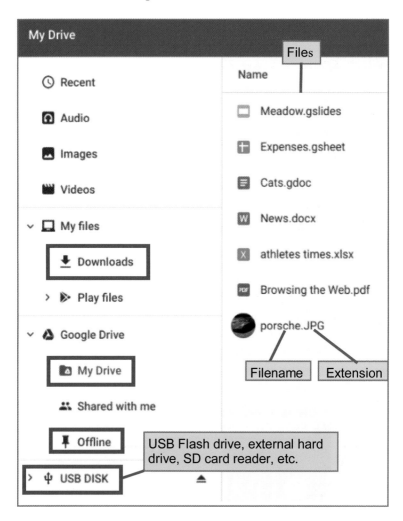

The four folders highlighted on page 94 are outlined briefly below and discussed in more detail in the rest of this chapter.

My Drive

All of the documents you create in Docs, Sheets and Slides are automatically saved in **My Drive** and constantly updated. Files in **My Drive** exist primarily on the Internet and can be viewed on any Internet computer, anywhere.

Downloads

This is Internal Storage used to keep files accessible only to your Chromebook, not on the Internet. Files can be downloaded to this folder from **My Drive**.

Offline

This is temporary storage allowing you to edit recent files when you have no Internet connection. Latest versions of files are uploaded to **My Drive** next time you go online.

USB DISK

External USB storage devices connected to the Chromebook's USB port appear here. Files such as photos and documents can be copied between the USB device and **My Drive** and the **Downloads** folder, as discussed below.

Copying and Downloading Files

Files can be copied between the various folders in the **Files** app by *dragging and dropping* the file, as discussed on page 20. Alternatively, *right-click* to select **Copy** from the menu which appears and then right-click again and select **Paste** as discussed on pages 19, 20 and 77.

My Drive

As shown on page 94, **My Drive** is part of **Google Drive**, the Google Internet Cloud Storage system. The documents, spreadsheets and slides you create with the Chromebook are automatically saved as *files* in the **My Drive** folder on the Internet

- You can access the **Drive** folder anywhere on any computer with an Internet connection — desktop, laptop, tablet or smartphone.

- To access the files in **My Drive** on any other online computer, open the Google website at:

    drive.google.com

- Sign in with your Google username and password, discussed on page 23 to start using files in **My Drive**.

- As shown on page 94, various Google *file types*, such as **gdoc**, **.gsheet**, **.gslides** can be created and saved in **My Drive**.

- Several other file types can be imported from other computers using removable storage such as USB flash drives and SD cards.

- Then they can be opened by double-clicking in the **Files** app for editing and printing in Docs, Sheets and Slides or moved between folders using drag and drop or cut/copy and paste.

- Compatible file types include Microsoft Word, Excel and PowerPoint, i.e..**docx**, **.xlsx**, **.pptx** respectively.

- Also **.pdf** and **.JPG** in the filename list on page 94 are widely used standard file types for text documents and photos respectively.

Printing a Document from My Drive

- Click **File** shown below to open the **File** menu including a **Print** option to click to print the document on paper. (Setting up a printer and other external devices is discussed later in this chapter.)

- In the example below, a Word Document has been opened for editing in Google Docs. There is also an option to save the Word **.docx** file in the Docs format.

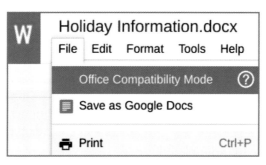

- Similarly there are **Save as Google Sheets** and **Save as Google Slides** options for Excel and PowerPoint files respectively.

My Drive Files Available Offline

Copies of your *recent* files are automatically *synced* from **My Drive** on the Internet to the **Offline** folder, shown on page 94. This is located on the *SSD* (*Solid State Drive)* inside the Chromebook. These files can be edited offline, so you can carry on working where there is no Internet.

Apart from recent files, you can make earlier files available for editing in the **Offline** folder. Simply right-click over the file in **My Drive** and select **Available offline** from the menu.

Deleting Temporary Offline Files

The Chromebook has limited internal storage, typically 16 or 32 GB. So temporary offline files should be deleted when they are no longer needed.

- Click in the **Status Area** at the bottom right of the screen, as shown on the right.

- Click the **Settings** icon shown on the right and on page 30 and 31. This opens the main **Settings** menu

- Scroll down and under **Device** select **Storage management**.

- Click the dustbin icon to the right of **Offline files** then click **Delete files** to remove temporary offline files. Files previously set as **Available offline** are not deleted.

Downloading in Different File Formats

The **Download as** option on the **File** menu in Google Docs, Sheets and Slides allows files created in Docs, Sheets and Slides to be saved in the **Downloads** folder in various formats, such as Word (**.docx**), Excel (**.xlsx**) and PowerPoint (**.pptx**) respectively. Files can also be downloaded in the popular **.pdf** format.

Download as ►	Microsoft Word (.docx)
Email as attachment...	OpenDocument format (.odt)
Version history ►	Rich Text Format (.rtf)
Rename...	PDF document (.pdf)

The Downloads Folder

- The **Downloads** folder outlined in red on page 94 is the local storage on your Chromebook's SSD. Files are not accessible to computers via the Internet.

- Files can be opened for editing offline by double-clicking the file name in the **Downloads** folder as shown below.

- Files can be copied between the **Downloads** folder and **My Drive** and to removable devices by dragging and dropping or cutting/copying and pasting as discussed on pages 77 and 95.

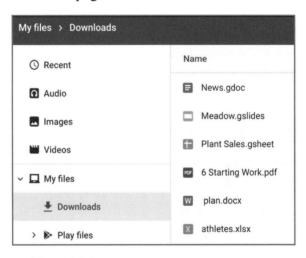

Creating a New Folder

To add a folder, (or a sub-folder within an existing folder) right-click in the **Name** column, as shown in the **Downloads** folder above. Then type a name and press **Enter** or **Return**.

Compatibility with Microsoft Office

- Microsoft Office files can be imported into **My Drive** from a USB external storage device. Microsoft Office files you create in My Drive on another computer are also accessible on your Chromebook.
- The files can be edited in Google Docs, Sheets and Slides after double-clicking the filename in **My Drive**.
- As shown for Word on page 97, there is an option to save Word, Excel and PowerPoint files in the Docs, Sheets and Slides file formats.

Microsoft Office Online

This is a free version of the Microsoft Office suite which runs as an *extension* in the Google Chrome browser.

- Search for **Office Online** in the Chrome Web Store.
- Click **Add to Chrome**.
- Click the icon, shown on the right and below at the top right of the Chrome screen.
- Sign in with a Microsoft account.
- Select Word, Excel, etc., to create or edit a document.

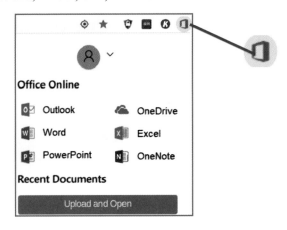

Getting Extra Storage in Google Drive

All users of Google Drive (on computers in general) are initially given 15GB of free Cloud Storage. However, at the time of writing, Chromebook users can claim an extra 100GB for 2 years, as follows:

- In Chrome, open the following website :
  google.com/chromebook/offers/
- Scroll down to **Google Drive** under **Latest Offers**.
- Click **Redeem** shown below.

- Click **Allow** so that Google can check that you are using a Chromebook and eligible for the offer.
- As mentioned on page 15, at the end of 2 years you need to make a monthly payment to continue with extra storage on **Google Drive**.
- Alternatively, after the 2 year period, delete files to remain within the standard 15GB of free storage.

Security of Your Files

The Chromebook is one of the most secure computers for the following reasons:

- Protection against malware is turned on by default.

- Viruses are small executable files or programs. These cannot be run on the Chromebook.

- Your files are *encrypted* to prevent illegal access.

- Security updates are automatically installed every few weeks.

- Each program runs in a *sandbox* or secure environment. Infected Web pages can't infect others.

- The *verified boot* checks the Chromebook on starting up to make sure it is secure and has not been attacked by hackers or malicious software.

- The files you create are automatically saved in **Google Drive** on server computers in the Clouds. So they are managed by professionals and should therefore be very secure.

Backup Copies

If you delete a file in **Google Drive**, either deliberately or accidentally, it's placed in the **Bin** shown on the right. You can *restore* deleted files from the **Bin** for a limited time, after which they are permanently removed.

So for important files, it's a good idea to make your own backup copies by dragging and dropping them onto removable USB storage such as flash drives and external hard drives, as discussed on page 17. Backup copies should be kept in a separate secure place.

Google Cloud Print

The Chromebook is not compatible with all printers. Google's solution is *Google Cloud Print*. This allows any computer, including the Chromebook, to print documents across the Internet to any printer, anywhere in the world.

If you already have a *Cloud Ready* printer, designed for printing across the Internet, this should be easy to set up for Cloud Print using the manufacturer's instructions.

A printer which is not Cloud Ready is known as a *classic* printer. This must be connected to a Windows PC or Mac on a *Wi-Fi network*. This computer must have Google Chrome installed and be signed in to your Google account.

On the Windows PC or Mac Computer

- Click the Chrome icon shown on the right.

- Click the 3-dot menu button and select **Settings**.

- Scroll down the screen and select **Advanced**.

- Scroll down again and under **Printing**, select **Google Cloud Print.**

- Select **Manage Cloud Print devices** and then select **Classic printers**. Select **Add printers**.

- Make sure the printer attached to the Windows PC or Mac is ticked and click **Add printer(s)**.

- A message should be displayed confirming that your printer is registered with Google Cloud Print.

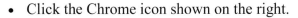

Google Cloud Print **Thanks, you're ready to start!**
Your printers are now registered with Google Cloud Print.
Manage your printers

On Your Chromebook

- Open a document you want to print in Docs or Sheets.
- Select **File** and **Print** or press **Ctrl+p**.

- If necessary click **Change** to select a different printer or **Destination** shown above.

- Finally click **Print** shown above to print the page(s).

USB Printing

Google Cloud Print just described is the most used method for Chromebook printing, enabling documents to be printed to any Cloud printer anywhere in the world.

It is possible to print from a Chromebook to a printer attached to the Chromebook by a USB cable but not all printers are compatible with the Chromebook. However, as Chromebooks become more popular, it is expected that more printer manufacturers will make sure their devices can print directly via a USB cable.

USB Connections

As discussed in Chapter 2, extra storage can be obtained by connecting flash drives, external hard drives and SD cards to the USB ports on Chromebooks. This may be useful if you are using the Chromebook where there is no Internet. For example if you are on a plane and want to read an ebook or watch a video. These external devices plug directly into a USB port as shown on page 13 or connect via a USB cable or *wireless dongle*. No setting up is required, the devices should be ready to use straightaway.

Once installed the USB storage devices are listed in the **Files** app, as shown below.

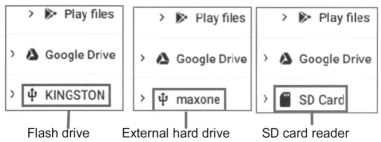

Flash drive   External hard drive   SD card reader   .

Instead of needing a removable SD card reader shown above, some Chromebooks have a built-in *SD card slot*.

Before removing a USB device, right click over its name in the **Files** app and click **Eject device** shown on the right. Otherwise the message **"Whoa, there. Be Careful"** pops up.

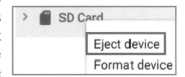

Separate mice and keyboards can also be connected to Chromebooks by USB cable or USB wireless dongle.

Using a Mobile Hotspot (Tethering)

Where there is no Wi-Fi or in an emergency, a smartphone can be used to connect a Chromebook to the Internet using the phone's 3G/4G (and soon 5G) wireless technology. Any browsing, etc., is charged against your phone's data plan.

Setting up a Moto G (5) smartphone is described in the cxample below. Other phones use similar methods.

- From the **Settings** menu on the smartphone, under **Network & Internet**, select **Mobile network** and make sure **Mobile data** is switched on.

- Under **Network & Internet** switch on **Hotspot & tethering** and then switch on **Wi-Fi hotspot** and select **Set up Wi-Fi hotspot** shown below on the left.

- Enter a **Password** for the hotspot, as shown below on the left, and tap **SAVE**.

- On the Chromebook, tap the Wi-Fi icon shown on the right and discussed on page 31.

- Select your phone from the Chromebook's list of available networks, as shown below on the right, including the **Moto G (5)** smartphone.

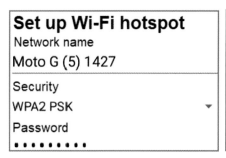

- **Connected** is then displayed under your phone's name in the list of Wi-Fi networks. The Chromebook now has access to the Internet via your smartphone.

Communication and Leisure

Introduction

This chapter shows how a Chromebook can be used to communicate with other people, using electronic mail and the Google Hangouts app. Leisure activities such as listening to music, watching TV and videos and reading eBooks are also discussed.

Electronic Mail

- Gmail is used for creating, sending and receiving text messages over the Internet.

- *Replies* can easily be sent to the sender of a message and to other recipients or *forwarded* to someone else.

- You set up an *address book* for all your contacts.

- An email message can include photos, documents, and other files, known as *attachments*.

- Your emails can be accessed from anywhere in the world using your Gmail user name and password.

Creating an Email

- Click the **Launcher** button or key shown on pages 18 and 26 to open the **ALL APPS** screen then click the Gmail icon shown on the right.

- Click **Compose** to start a **New Message**, as shown on the next page.

- Enter the recipient's email address and the subject before typing the text of the message.

- Click **Cc** and **Bcc** to send *carbon copies* or *blind carbon copies* to other recipients. The **Bcc** recipients are not visible to the other recipients.

- To add an attachment, such as a photo or document, etc., click the paperclip icon shown below. Then browse to find and click the file, then click **OPEN**.

- Finally click **Send**.

Receiving an Email

- The email is listed in the recipient's *Inbox*.

- They will see the sender's name and the text and any photos, listed by name as shown above.

- To open an attached document or photo, tap its file name.

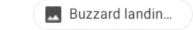

- Tap the star icon to mark the email as a *favourite*. The star changes to yellow.

- Click the buttons, as shown below, to reply to the sender or forward the message to someone else.

Google Hangouts

Some of the main features of Hangouts, pre-installed on a new Chromebook, are:

- Communicating with individuals and groups of up to 10 people.
- Sharing free voice and video calls.
- Instant messaging, including photos and emojis.
- Viewing a list of your missed calls and messages.
- Compatibility with various types of computer.

Launching Hangouts

- Click the **Launcher** button or key shown on pages 18 and 26 to open the **ALL APPS** screen then click the Hangouts icon shown on the right.

- Click **New conversation**.

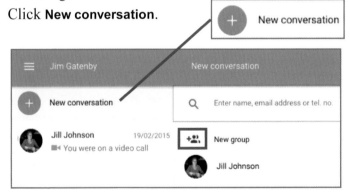

- Listed on the left above are your previous calls, etc. Your contacts are listed on the right as well as an icon to start a **New group**, by entering names, email addresses and telephone numbers.

- Click one of the four icons below to start a call or message.

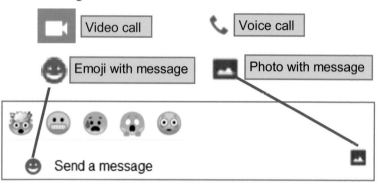

- Click **Allow** to let Hangouts use your microphone and camera.

- The person receiving the call can either **ANSWER** or **DECLINE**. A video call in progress is shown below.

- More contacts (who must have the Hangouts app installed) can be invited to join in after clicking the icon shown on the right and below.

Play Books

- Open the **ALL APPS** screen, as discussed on page 109 and click the Play Books icon shown on the right. There are 3 main screens, as shown below:

- The **Home** screen opens on startup showing books recommended for you. Click either **Ebooks** or **Audiobooks** at the top of the screen.

- Click **Shop** shown above to display books in categories, e.g. **Top selling**, **Genres**, **Comics**, etc.

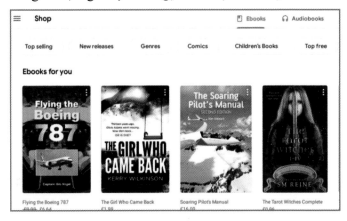

- Click on a book to read details and click again to read sample pages. Then click again if you wish to buy it.

- Clicking **Library** shown above displays all the books you've bought or downloaded for free. Click a book in the **Library** to start reading it.

Play Music

This app on the **ALL APPS** screen is similar to Play Books and allows you to shop for and buy music in various categories and add them to your music **Library**.

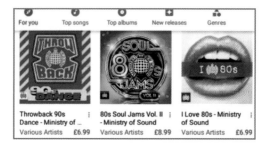

To play a tune, click the Play Music icon shown at the top right above and select the menu button shown right and click **Music library**. Click the song and then click the **Play** button shown on the right.

Play Movies & TV

This app lets you rent or buy films and TV programs in a range of categories, as shown in the sample below.

YouTube

Click the YouTube icon shown on the right to view a huge range of videos uploaded by various people.

Connecting a Chromebook to a Large Screen

- The Chromebook screen can be mirrored to a monitor or TV, for making a slide presentation to an audience, showing photos or streaming videos, etc.

- An *HDMI* cable may be used to connect the Chromebook's *HDMI* port (shown on page 13) to an HDMI port on the monitor or TV.

- The *input channel* on a TV has to be set to the HDMI port to which the cable is attached to the TV.

- An *HDMI to VGA* adapter cable can be used to connect the HDMI port on the Chromebook to a monitor or TV with a VGA port.

- Select **Settings > Device > Displays** and make sure **Mirror Internal Display** is ticked and also that **Mirrored** appears in a box, as shown below on the right..

☑ Mirror Internal Display   Mirrored

Shown below is a Chromebook screen mirrored to a VGA monitor.

Bluetooth

Many Chromebooks have built-in *Bluetooth* short-range wireless technology. This is used to connect Bluetooth devices such as speakers and headphones.

Pairing Two Bluetooth Devices

- Bluetooth should be **On** in the Chromebook's **Settings** as shown on pages 30 and 31.

- Follow the manufacturer's instructions to enable the Chromebook to discover the Bluetooth device.

- Under **Unpaired devices** in the Chromebook **Settings,** select the device you want to connect, such as the headphones, **SX16** in this example. The connection process begins as shown below. You may be asked to check that the same PIN number appears on both devices.

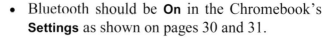

Pair Bluetooth device

Connecting to 'SX16'

- After a short time, the device should be listed as **Connected** under **Paired devices**, as shown below. It is now ready to be used by the Chromebook.

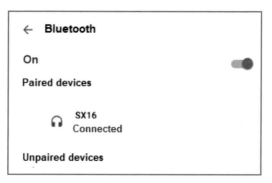

← **Bluetooth**

On

Paired devices

SX16
Connected

Unpaired devices

Index